My LORD His Adversary

To: Ms Williams

God Bless You.

MINISTERS DARREN AND ASHARAN PAUL

authorHOUSE®

AuthorHouse™
1663 Liberty Drive, Suite 200
Bloomington, IN 47403
www.authorhouse.com
Phone: 1-800-839-8640

First published by AuthorHouse   11/13/2007

ISBN: 978-1-4343-4744-2 (sc)

Printed in the United States of America
Bloomington, Indiana

This book is printed on acid-free paper.

TABLE OF CONTENTS

Acknowledgements

First and foremost we give our continuous thanks, glory and honor unto God who is the Head of our lives and with this, has challenged us through times of joy, and especially in the midst of adversity, to give *Him* the opportunity to show us why He truly is, the most awesome, loving, and irreplaceable God to ever be in this world. We love You and *without* You, this would have never been possible.

We also thank God for our three sons, Diaje, Darian and Judah Paul, who have inspired us to fight for what we believe in, and for showing us their unconditional love throughout every situation that we have experienced together. May Gods' love and protection, always abide with you, all the days of your lives; we love you *always*.

We would also like to express our appreciation to those who particularly supported and encouraged us during this spiritual journey. Those persons particularly are: Edward & Dorothy Prosper, Harold & Ivamae, Christopher and Mark Adderley and

Stephanie Mackey, Ministers Christopher & Ethel Wommack, Shawn & Felicia Bastian, Christopher Gilbert, Prophetess Dina Rolle, Geleta Washington, Sean "Go Go" Gomez, Tamika Bowe, Minister Deborah McFall, Pastor Louis Jones, Royanne "Roya" Williamson, Dwight, Dwight Jr. and Destinique Rahming, Verneice Grant, Nelson Lord, Brent & Anna Withers, David Spzond and to everyone else who we may not have mentioned, but have also poured unconditional love into our lives, and helped us to keep moving forward with what we believe.

Finally, we show a special appreciation to Joseph Pugh, Dawn Bowe, Jody Scipio and Brian Sampson, for assisting us and mostly for supporting our vision. Last, but definitely not least, to Maureen Golden and the entire Management & Production Team at Author House, for making this project *truly* special, and a memorable legacy that will be cherished for years to come.

We thank God for all of you, collectively and individually; as each one of you possessed a unique attribute that gave us the chance to stay motivated, by believing in ourselves, and in our dreams.

GODS BLESSINGS TO YOU ALL!

DEDICATION

In loving memory of
Linda C. Prosper-Ferguson and Nicola P. Rahming

Whose love can *never* be replaced and neither
forgotten.
May His Peace, be with you both, 'til we meet
again.

**Love always, your son and brother,
Darren a.k.a 'Dede'**

PREFACE

This book is an insight to everyday thinking. It is about questions that everyday people ask, and no one is around to answer them. Some of those questions are: Does God really exist, or is He just a figment of our imagination? Is there really a Heaven and a Hell?

This book will also tackle those mind boggling questions that most would avoid, and at the same time, it provides answers to those questions. For example, what actually happened before this earth was created?

It explores the depths of the Caveman Age in connection to the time of the Creation. It also discusses the life of Adam and Eve, whilst placing these two theories: the Caveman Age and Adam and Eve, on one platform.

This book may or may not be accurate to some, but it is just another perspective on some of life's greatest theories.

While reading this book, we ask that you would please open your mind to the possibilities of the unknown and the unimaginable. It is with our sincere request that we humbly ask and pray, that *you* would pray to the Creator / the One True God, before reading any further into this book. Solely for your guidance, and that you may receive a full understanding from and through the revelation that is given here, in order to unlock the hidden mysteries that await you.

Fact, fiction or truth? You decide.

"But God hath revealed *them* unto us by His Spirit: for the Spirit searcheth all things, yea, the **deep** things *of* **God.**

For what man knoweth the things of a man, save the spirit of a man which is in him? even so the things of God knoweth no man, but the Spirit of God.
Now we have received, not the spirit of the world, but the Spirit which is of God; **that we might know the things that are freely given to us of God.**"
1 Corinthians 2: 10-12

"But speak thou the things which **<u>become</u>** sound doctrine"

Titus 2:1

Chapter 1 – Who is God?

This is a question frequently asked amongst most individuals; a question that is sometimes misunderstood and even overlooked. It is constantly explored because we are not and never will be oblivious to the fact that we did not just emerge from nothing. In our opinion it is only fair to say that since nothing plus nothing equals nothing, **everything** that *exists* does not just explode or wills itself into being.
So where *do* we begin?

Perhaps it is somewhat easier to say that God is the Author of the best selling novel ever written. He is the Creator of <u>all</u> things that exist, which makes Him, Alpha and Omega, the Beginning and the End. (**Revelations 1:8**) We could say this and leave it at that point, but your question would then be, how do you know for sure that God really is the one and *only* true God? Let us now explore the possibilities of why God *is* God, and why He is the *only* true and living God.

As we mentioned earlier, nothing plus nothing equals nothing. This shows us that you truly had to have a point to begin. Therefore; we must have something to begin from in order for us to have a beginning and an end. We will begin to explore who God truly is and what makes all others incomparable to Him; by first briefly mentioning some of these religions who either do not or do worship other gods to be that of, or give the essence of an immortal being and/or force and their beliefs.

❖ Islam – This religion believes that Allah is god alone, which makes it monotheistic; and Muhammad (a descendant from the prophet Ishmael, who is the son of the prophet Abraham) was his last Messenger. It is believed that Allah had also transmitted knowledge through (those who are regarded as) prophets such as: Adam, Abraham, Moses and Jesus. Those revelations that were given to these prophets can be found in the Holy Quran, which denotes that of the Islamic lifestyle and culture.

❖ Buddhism – This religion does not believe in a Divine being, but rather in Buddha (who was named Siddhartha Guatama from birth and) who is seen as "the enlightened one". His teachings involve that of the physical and spiritual discipline that liberates all from this world's suffering, which is brought on by each individual's personal desires (e.g. hate, greed, etc.). Once this discipline is attained through the continuous process of reincarnation, it will bring forth the state of nirvana to that individual.

❖ Chinese Folk Religion – This religion is comprised of gods, goddesses, saints, immortals and demigods. These deities are recognized in legends, festivals, worship and various devotions; and are associated with the Chinese culture in a mythological aspect.

❖ Shamanism – This religion believes that Shamans are the "priests, priestess, or mediums" who possess special powers which allows them to communicate and influence ancestral spirits, the gods, or their evil counterparts. This belief is also extended to that of animism, deities and demons.

❖ Atheism – Although it is not perceived as a religion, the overall belief in this aspect is that there is no God; neither did any God or gods exist. The main objective is that an individual's life should be carried out based on their personal view of proper conduct.

❖ Judaism – This religion shares a great deal of teachings which are similar to those as in Christianity. However; it is monotheistic, because they do not believe that their god comprises of a three part divinity or anything else for that matter. Instead, he alone is the only god that exists.

❖ Sikhism - This religion which is also monotheistic, have beliefs that state their god cannot take on human form and that his identity remains unknown. His disciples, once they live and remain righteous in accordance to the 10 Gurus teachings that are found in the Sikh Holy Bible and the Living Guru, and they reject rituals, distinctions, idolatry and asceticism; they will then be brought forth to a state, whereby they will be merged with their god.

❖ Shintoism – This Japanese religion involved the worship (in the past days and scarcely found in some areas in this day) of kami – (which is sometimes translated to be "god" or "deity") spirits; whereas some kami are local and can be regarded as the spiritual being or genius of a particular place, but other ones represent major natural objects and processes. Shintoism also carries an animistic belief system.

❖ Spiritism (Spiritualism) – This religion observes the belief of the human souls surviving the state of death, whereas they communicate with the living by means of a "sensitive" medium. These mediums are able to demonstrate all psychic powers, which are specifically: clairvoyance, clairaudience, telekinesis and telepathy.

❖ Taoism (Daoism) – Tao is defined as "path" or "road", and it gives the belief that "it" (Tao) is a force that flows through all life. One can experience a wholesome and fulfilling life once it is in accordance with the philosophy of Taoism and nature. However; there are no deities.

❖ Wicca – This religion carries many varieties of witchcraft that are founded on religious and magical concepts. Wicca is seen to be neopagan and is also duo theistic; which gives to them two deities who are more specifically, the god which is symbolized by the sun and the goddess which is symbolized by the moon. Both are equal to each other and are recognized by a variety of names, depending solely on the situation that one is being faced with. They are sometimes called "The All" or "The One", and the prayers that are made, regard them to be the "Guardians" of the North, South, East and West.

When we look at these and many other religions, many of their beliefs are either targeted towards worshipping gods who are linked to mythologies, those that believe the universal energies alone in this world, are the human means of allowing life to function in such a manner, that the human mindset will gradually come to accept the natural flow of their "life" and everything that occurs on its own; and even those beliefs that are connected to mortal gods/goddess or messiahs, who are purposed to uplift mankind and represent a higher way of life whether in a past, present and/or futuristic era. However; although these gods, energy forces and all other types of religious beliefs are believed to emit a greater sense of spirituality; when they are placed on a platform next to God who is also known as "Jehovah" or "Yahweh", there truly is *no* comparison.

The history of this world shows amongst the many different races and nationalities throughout time, that whenever God was "experienced" in the full sense of the word, regardless of that individuals' lifestyle and culture, **all** are transformed new.

God is the *only* God who can for example, take a complete stranger from a place in this world that you have never been to in your *entire* life, and bring them to "you". With this, He can then have them reveal (if He wills) the most private and personal events of your life that only you alone would know; and can then have that person show you the relevance of how God alone, can take that pain or devastation of whatever may have affected you from that time, and truly give you "beauty for ashes" if you allow Him to do so. (Isaiah 61:3)

He *is* the only God who is able to take a person who is infected with any type of illness; have issued, doctor reports proving them to be positive of this disease, and on command, within seconds, cause that person's body to be healed from the inside out, without leaving a trace of evidence. God is "in fact" the only God, who can show up at the very last moment before something tragic is about to take place and deliver you from that situation without you even receiving such as a scratch from whatever you were facing; and this we can personally attest to with all confidence.

God does things that are humanly *impossible,* and with that, "the impossible and unthinkable" goes beyond the natural realm of our understanding. This is by the simple fact that only He alone can walk into time and turn any situation around, show up "on time" when there appears to be no time left, and mostly, He is not and never will be limited *to* time. This and so much more, shows that He is the God we all (knowingly and unknowingly) seek to find.

He defines Himself, and with this exquisite ability to be omnipresent, omniscient, omnipotent and eternal, in our opinion, this clarifies how it *is* possible for Him to exist before this world or anything for that matter, came to be. This is because He is the immortal invisible; comprised of God the Father, God the Son and God the Holy Spirit, who is better known as "the Holy Trinity", without question and beyond all levels of understanding. But nonetheless, we feel that because He is *not* visible to the physical state, this depicts why many have come to misunderstand Him. In observing the marvelous aspects of creation, the universe and even beyond, where then can we honestly say that these other gods come close to having this same ability? We believe that there is no other God, and this is by no means of disrespect to those of you, who have chosen to believe otherwise. In all truth, there has been none that reveals this type of groundbreaking evidence, even to this very day.

"For the invisible things of Him from the creation of the world are clearly seen, being understood by the things that are made, *even* His eternal power and Godhead; so that they are without excuse"
Romans 1:20

God *is* more specifically, Jehovah-Jireh (the Lord will Provide), Jehovah-Nissi (The Lord our Banner), Jehovah-Tsidkenu (the Lord our Righteousness), Jehovah-Shalom (The Lord our Peace), Jehovah–Rophe (The Lord Who Heals), Jehovah-Rohi (The Lord our Shepherd), Jehovah-M'Kaddesh (The Lord who Sanctifies), Jehovah-Sabaoth (the Lord of Hosts), Jehovah-Shammah (The Lord is There), El-Elyon (Most High God and the Exalted One), El-Berith (God of the covenant), El-Gibhor (God the Warrior), El-Shaddai (God all Sufficient), Kadosh (The Holy One of Israel), Adonai (Lord & Master) and *so* much more. All this shows how there will never be any circumstance that someone may face, and He is not able to be the God who will inevitably, reign and rule in that circumstance once their trust is placed in Him alone. He is Sovereign and irreplaceable, and as He stated to the children of

Israel in the book of Exodus and even now to us in this day, "I AM *that* I AM." For all of this, He **truly** is and will always be all that you *ever* will need.

Now that we know who God is and what makes Him, God all by Himself; let us examine the **natural** evidence to our human design which causes us to not only know that He is "in fact" our Creator; but also come to recognize that He has brought into existence that which can only be fathomed to perform (by men) and by all means, that of a distinguished brilliance.

Take for instance the mere fact that humans are created at first from a zygote, this being a single-cell organism, made up of genetic DNA material from both father and mother; which then continues this unique process of division and is comprised with an evenly divided number of chromosomes, 23 from each parent, giving 46 in total. These chromosomes begin what can only be described as the miracle of life in itself. The structure that is formed hence creates a unique and individualized formation that in just 40 weeks, gives over to the complete development of a fully functional human being, who will, remarkably, never again be replicated after its' kind.

This ingenious design speaks for itself and in essence, the vast majority of all things reproduced inevitably will carry the similarities if not identical to this same pattern. So by examining this amongst everything else, it shows that, everything created down to the human race is therefore designed. Moreover, in saying this, if there is a design which has already been proven, there *has* to be a Designer.

Another example is with the car that you drive now; it was taken from the very first gas automobile that was designed in the year 1878 by Karl Friedrich Benz and now years later, today you have millions of cars that are designed in every size, shape and fashion, all over the world. Once again, when you search history, you will come to discover that it states, Karl Friedrich Benz is the original designer of the gas automobile after the given prototypes of first the steam vehicle and then the electric carriage. So even though you have many variations of car types, it all boils back down to the original designer of automobiles or the motorcar himself, from whence all these came.

This in itself, gives more than sound proof that we are not just incidental as the Big Bang Theory suggests, We *are* a design that illustrates we came from a Designer. But how we are created amongst all other creations shows that we are not only unique, but we have similarities to our Creator that truly makes us one of a kind. Refer to the scripture given:

"And God said, Let us make man in our image, after our likeness: and let them have dominion over the fish of the sea, and over the fowl of the air, and over the cattle, and over all the earth, and over every creeping thing that creepeth upon the earth. So God created man in His *own* image, in the image of God created He him; male and female created He them."

Genesis 1:26-27

Unknown gods

However; although it is ever so commonly and easily overlooked, we at times can get so caught up in our own daily agendas, that we can unknowingly acquire what is also known as "a god or an idol". You may ask, how is this possible? Well, let's take for example; someone purchases a home or a car, or it can be where that person has become the focus of their own attention. They don't necessarily just like this particular item or themselves to what is considered reasonable; they adore it or themselves *so* much to a point, where they will do things that aren't common to the "average" person.

They may do certain things such as obsessing over its or their beauty, constantly bragging on what they or it means to them. It may even get to a point where they are often over-protective of how others handle such in their presence. i.e. "Don't touch it like that! You're too close, move back a little!" These things can, and often do lead to worshipping what is now known as a **god** or an **idol**. So with saying this, let's take a closer look to what scripture states on this area:-

"Because that, when they knew God, they glorified *Him* not as God, neither were thankful; but became vain in their imaginations, and their foolish heart was darkened.

Professing themselves to be wise, they became fools, And changed the glory of the uncorruptible God into an image made like to corruptible man, and to birds and four-footed beasts and creeping things. Wherefore God also gave them up to uncleanness through the lusts of their own hearts, to dishonor their own bodies between themselves: Who changed the truth of God into a lie, and worshipped and served the creature more rather than the Creator, who is blessed for ever."

Romans 1:21-25

This clearly gives reason to why many persons today are lost, confused and are filling the void in their lives with vanity and idolatry, rather than filling that spot with what it was purposed to be filled with, that, being God, who *is* the lover of your soul, and who alone can and *will* give you that complete and endless joy and happiness that we all long and seek after.

Unforeseen dangers from serving other gods

Amongst everything that has been mentioned, we must know and not forget the severity of those repercussions that comes from worshipping these other gods. The Bible clearly states repeatedly throughout different books, the dangers in being ignorant and careless of placing gods or idols, in the place where only God aught to be. In Exodus 20, given in the 10 Commandments that were sent directly from God through the hand of Moses, to the children of Israel; He commands and also warns specifically what you should not do and why you should not do it. Let's examine the scripture as given below:

"And God spake all these words, saying, I *am* the LORD thy God, which have brought thee out of the land of Egypt, out of the house of bondage. Thou shalt have no other gods before me. Thou shalt not make unto thee any graven image, or any likeness *of any thing* that *is* in heaven above, or that *is* in the earth beneath, or that *is* in the water under the earth: Thou shalt not bow down thyself to them, nor serve them: for I the LORD thy God *am* a jealous God, visiting the iniquity of the fathers upon the children unto the third and fourth *generation* of them that hate me; And

showing mercy unto thousands of them that love me, and keep My commandments."

Exodus 20:1-6

God makes it perfectly clear that He *is* God, and that no one will ever take His place. If it is by chance attempted by man, or anything for that matter or is placed there by the same, He will "utterly destroy" that particular thing or person whatever it may be, and not in a sense that denotes where a person *will* be brought to a physical death. As we have experienced with many persons in our past, that did the same that He speaks against; they were more or less brought down, and the things that they held dear to them and worshipped for that much besides God, were then destroyed and ceased to exist with them as it once was.

It is also mentioned that He will visit **"the iniquity of the fathers upon the children unto the third and fourth generation of them that hate Me."** This may or may not bring some confusion to you, however; we will give a brief clarity on what revelation is given on this scripture. We are often fond of the term **curse**, and we usually link them to spells that have been cast or to some unforeseen spiritual presence that has decided to plague us. Although some of these claims can be linked to truthful sources in their origins, we however; must understand the true source of this word. It was hence given to these mentioned, who were then or still were hateful towards God. With this, God "visiting the iniquity" or sin as what it is based from, carries on to say He will do just that, up to the third and fourth generation. This is where **generational curses** comes into play, and it carries a great deal of evidence as to why many have been and still are plagued in a particular manner, even to this present day.

Countless are not knowledgeable of this truth or they simply don't believe that it truly can carry that much of an effect, and unfortunately, it is not regarded highly among many in this day and time. According to the Bible, whether it is believed or not, it is and will always remain true. The Bibles' word has been tried and tested by many through out history and is still proven effective today.

To gain a more in depth study on these generational curses, we recommend that you read **"Unbroken Curses" by Rebecca Brown MD and Daniel Yoder**, where you will receive a better insight to the weights this unforeseen dilemma causes and carries in families, societies and even some cultures.

Finally in saying all of this, we also would like to take note of the last but not least portion of the scripture that is mentioned. As it states:

"And showing mercy unto thousands of them that love me, and keep My commandments".

Exodus 20:6

This is for those of you out there who have been reading this chapter so far, and may have begun to feel some sense of uncompromising anger and control from God. He however; being a God of unconditional love and compassion, will always give mercy unto those who seek after Him in all spirit and in truth. He gives a promise of compassion, mercy, and faithful love to you once you obey Him and keep His commandments.

We would also like to take this time to briefly mention that too many of you out there who are either unbelievers, atheist's or simply those of you who are unaware of God's infinite mercy towards humanity, believe that God is for some reason, seen as a force that cannot be understood and His ways seem to be almost ancient and too unrealistic. But from the outside looking in on this situation, we are too often mislead by the things of this world or other devices sent from the enemy, Satan (who will be further discussed later in the book) to keep us distracted from knowing who God really is to us. When you have finally stopped and taken the time to give Him a chance and allow God to reveal Himself to you, you will not only find how truly awesome He is and can become in your life, but you will also unlock the key to finding all of your dreams and hearts desires.

Although strangely but true, you *will* come to discover with time, once you have been re-connected with the One who purposed your creation, that you will then see where you have unlocked the person who you were *truly* destined to become. You may also find yourself, seeing the "old you", really didn't have much, if any *real* appeal at all and that you were possibly fooling yourself all along. But don't just take our word for it, give it a try; with all the decisions that you will make in a life time, give "yourself" a chance to discover God, and in essence we can guarantee, granted you remain focused, that you *will* discover your **true self**; what would be better known as "a Diamond in the rough."

So really, what *do* you have to lose?

CHAPTER 2 – THE DWELLING PLACE OF THE MOST HIGH

When the word Heaven is mentioned, what comes to your mind? (Think about it for a moment)

Do you begin to think of great waterfalls that are crystal clear cascading near to a road paved with gold and diamonds? Do you imagine perhaps, the clouds are all arrayed white and with a magnificent light overpowering the entire scenery, making it humanly impossible to behold such glory? Well, however you decide it may be, and although for many reasons its complete state may just remain a mystery until the appointed time, the truth of the matter is that, Heaven is physically to us, the visible firmament; but from the *spiritual* aspect, there are parts that we may not even realize exist right in front of us that are unseen for that matter.

Now, how is this possible? First let us explore some of the definitions of these two (2) words, **Heaven** & **Firmament**:

- ❖ **Heaven** – (according to The New American Webster Dictionary Third Edition) as given in its fourth definition, describes this as "the visible sky; the firmament."

- ❖ **Firmament** – (From the same reference) as defined means "the visible sky; the heavens."

After examining all of this, we have realized that the Bible states in Genesis 1:1, "In the beginning God created the heaven and the earth." The key word here is **created**. Why then, would God have to create someplace that He supposedly, already dwells in? This poses a contradiction in itself. So, how *can* one "create" a place somewhere that they already reside in? This simply does not make any sense, therefore; this in itself gives evidence to show that God does not dwell or reside in Heaven. Let's read closely to what the scripture states in regards to heaven, as given below:

"And I saw a new heaven and a new earth: for the first heaven and the first earth were passed away; and there was no more sea. And I John saw the holy city, new Jerusalem, coming down from God out of heaven, prepared as a bride adorned for her husband."

Revelation 21:1-2

We see here that the first heaven and the first earth had passed away, meaning that they ceased to exist. Our earth as we know it now, is actually in a state where by this "passing away" in that sense, is essential and makes perfect sense to be ridden of for its' calamity and sinful state.

You may ask, how is it that God would want to get rid of the place where He supposedly dwells; that place being heaven and bring forth a *new* heaven? Why is this necessary? This would then, cause one to wonder is this *really* where He dwells since He is holy and without blemish? If this is so, why fix something that is not broken? God has no need to improve this place because He is already perfect and where He is must be the same.

"*He is* the Rock, His work *is* perfect: for all His ways *are* judgment: a God of truth and without iniquity, just and right *is* He."

Deuteronomy 32:4

This scripture gives reference to what is being said here. God *is* perfect and where He **dwells** is also perfect. So given that He being perfect, will only dwell in the same conditions, why would He then, destroy this perfect place?

Although, it is not mentioned directly in the beginning of the Bible, God dwelt in a place known as "the holy city", or better known as the Kingdom of Heaven/ Kingdom of God.

You may now ask, "How can we be so certain of this specific dwelling place for God?" Given for your reference on this subject, are a few scriptures noted below for your personal review. These are scriptures where Jesus spoke many times about this dwelling place in the gospels as well as in a number of other books found in the New Testament:

Matthew 18:3, Mark 9:47, Luke 9:62, John 3:3-5, Acts 14:22, 1 Corinthians 6:9-10, 1 Corinthians 15:50 and Galatians 5:21.

Now, if you recall earlier in the scripture that was mentioned, Revelation 21:2 states:

"And I John saw the holy city, new Jerusalem, coming down from God out of heaven."

God releases this city from heaven, that being from out of the firmament or sky. So let us rephrase this scripture by taking out the word **heaven** and replacing it with the word **sky**. Behold, how it now changes the perception of this scripture:

Revelation 21:1 **"And I saw a new (sky)** heaven **and a new earth: for the first (sky)** heaven **and the first earth were passed away; and there was no more sea."**

Revelation 21:2 **"And I John saw the holy city, new Jerusalem, coming down from God out of the**

(sky) heaven, **prepared as a bride adorned for her husband."**

Now do the same with the following scriptures:-

"In the beginning God created the <u>heaven</u> and the earth."

Genesis 1:1

"And there came a voice from <u>heaven</u>, *saying*, Thou art my beloved Son, in whom I am well pleased.

Mark 1:11

"And when He had taken the five loaves and the two fishes, He looked up to <u>heaven</u>, and blessed, and brake the loaves, and gave *them* to His disciples to set before them; and the two fishes divided He among them all."

Mark 6:41

"So then after the Lord had spoken unto them, He was received up into <u>heaven</u>, and sat on the right hand of God."

Mark 16:19

So now that we are placing heaven and sky together as well as showing you where they are connected; it makes sense to see that God being omnipresent *is* in heaven and earth, however; He dwells in a specific place (Zechariah 2:13) in which He will come to bring His chosen to be with Him at an appointed time. Nonetheless to relate all of the evidence that is given here, God Himself states in Genesis 1:8 **"And God called the firmament (or the sky) Heaven"**.

Now that we have gained a better understanding to what this all means, let us now see why it is necessary for God to destroy this present heaven and bring forth a new one.

"Wherein in time past ye walked according to the course of this world, according to the prince of the power of the air (Satan), the spirit that now worketh in the children of disobedience."
Ephesians 2:2

"For we wrestle not against flesh and blood, but against principalities, against powers, against the rulers of the darkness of the world, <u>against spiritual wickedness in *high places*</u>."
Ephesians 6:12

We realize now that the prince of the power of the "air" is not only in the earth, but also in the heavens (which is the sky). So in order to get rid of all evil in both places, God *must* destroy the first heaven and the first earth. Take note of what is being said specifically in this scripture given:

"And there was war in heaven: Michael and his angels fought against the dragon; and the dragon fought and his angels, And prevailed not; neither was their place found any more in heaven."

Revelation 12:7-8

Here it shows specifically that their "place" being in heaven or in the sky, is brought to an end. This gives awareness that even at this very same moment, until that appointed time, these rulers of darkness have their positions still being maintained, but not under the direction of God. Evil is evidently and actively moving in our world today, whether it is seen or unseen.

The Holy Angels

We have now established the basic understanding of Heaven and the actual dwelling place of God, now to which we will explore the holy angels that dwelt in the presence of God and specify their duties to which God has given them under certain levels of authority through out the Kingdom of Heaven/ God.

It was said by Dionysius (A pre-500 A.D. writer) that there are three (3) hierarchies, which are grouped in each three specific orders of angels, where each order carries out separate duties. However; the Bible gives no specific reference to any rankings or orders for that much, but there are references made to the types mentioned as follows:

❖ Seraphim – They are known to be positioned above or over the throne of God according to Isaiah 6:1-4; and give continuous praise & worship unto God. They are depicted as "each one had six wings; with twain he covered his face, and with twain he covered his feet, and with twain he did fly." However; in this specific scripture, it is not mentioned as to what the other possible physical characteristics of the seraphim were. Along with this, some (once reading this description) might think the Seraphim's were either covering themselves or covering the appearance of God; as there is no capitalization regarded towards God in this scripture to bring clarity. Instead, it is shown as "his" rather than "His" in Isaiah chapter 6 and verse 2. Nonetheless, we would rather believe that it is "in fact" Gods' presence that is being covered since it is shown in the Bible where Gods' face was not revealed to man, but only that of His glory. (Exodus 33: 12-23 & Job 19:26).

❖ Cherubim – These are known to dwell closest or surround the throne of God according to the following scriptures: 2 Samuel 6:2,

2 Kings 19:15, 1 Chronicles 28:18, Psalms 80:1 & 99:1 and Ezekiel 1:5-12 & 10:1-22. They are depicted in scripture as "They had the likeness of a man. And every one having four faces, and every one had four wings, And their feet *were* straight feet; and the sole of their feet *was* like the sole of a calf's foot: and they sparkled like the colour of burnished brass. And *they had* the hands of a man under their wings on their four sides; and they four had their faces and their wings. Their wings were joined one to another; As for the likeness of their faces, they four had the face of a man, and the face of a lion, on the right side: and they four had the face of an ox on the left side; they four also had the face of an eagle. Their wings *were* stretched upward; two *wings* of every one *were* joined one to another, and two covered their bodies." This depiction may bring some difficulty to imagine, however; we must remember that Gods' ways and thoughts are higher than ours; and their ultimate purpose in the Kingdom is far beyond that what can be understood by the human mind.

❖ Thrones (also known as "Wheels" or "Having Many Eyes") – These are known to be assigned one to each cherub, and are near below to the throne of God according to Ezekiel 1:16-25 & 10:9-10 and Colossians 1:16. They also appear on the lower parts of the throne of God, close near to the cherubim and are depicted through scripture as "the living creatures (that) ran and returned as the appearance of a flash of lightning. The appearance of the wheels was as the color of a beryl stone: and they four had one likeness, as if a wheel had been in the midst of a wheel. As their whole body, and their backs, and their hands, and their wings and the wheels, *were* full of eyes round about, even the wheels that they four had"

❖ Dominions – These are not depicted as far as scripture states, but they are mentioned in the scriptures Daniel 7:27 and Colossians 1:16.

❖ Powers – These are not depicted as far as scripture states, but these are mentioned in the scriptures Romans 8:38 & 13:1, Ephesians 3:10 & 6:12, Colossians 1:16 and 1Peter 3:22.

❖ Principalities – These are not depicted as far as scripture states, but they are mentioned in the scriptures Romans 8:38, Ephesians 3:10

& 6:12 and Colossians 1:16 & 2:15.

❖ Archangels – There is no other specific archangel recognized other than Michael "the archangel" who is mentioned twice in the scriptures 1 Thessalonians 4:16 and Jude 1:9. Michael whose name means "who is like God" however; is also mentioned in scripture according to Daniel 10: 10-13 to be "one of the chief princes." We may assume that he *is* the leader of the archangels (and angels) because of what scriptures states in Revelation 12:7. Although, there is no complete Biblical evidence given that Michael is the *only* head or leading archangel for that matter, Michael is known to be a warrior angel, but also one who reveals Gods will to His people. There are depictions made of angels however; none has shown in scripture specifically, depictions made of the archangel.

❖ Angels/ Ministering Spirits – There are a great number of Biblical references that are given to these; some can be found in the following scriptures: Judges 6:21-22, Mark 1:13, Luke 1:26, Hebrews 1:13-14, Galatians 1:8 and Revelation 5:2 & 7:2. They bring forth the word from God, as Messengers, and administer to those in need of protection and guidance on earth. There are some depictions given, but one more specifically is in Daniel 10:4-6. However; there are numerous occasions in the Bible where people have seen angels, whereas some describe them to have the appearance of a man; though there is no evidence by scripture to guarantee that they all have one specific or similar appearance.

❖ Fallen Angels / Demonic Spirits – These are angels that were once holy but sinned against God and have in result of this, lost their positions in the Kingdom of Heaven/God. These angels were involved in the fall of Satan and made up the 1/3, that were thrown down from the Kingdom of Heaven/God here to earth. (2 Peter 2:4 and Revelation 12:4). They are given specifically as stated in Ephesians 6:12 as shown below:

"For we wrestle not against flesh or blood; but against **principalities**, against **powers**, against the rulers of the darkness of this world, against spiritual wickedness in high places."

The use of their previous authority and powers are now completely geared towards evil and are evident in many situations mentioned in the New Testament of the Bible. Some of these are shown in scriptures such as Luke 8:26-39 where Jesus heals a man from a legion of demons, and also in Acts 19:13-16 where some **unsaved** persons made an attempt to cast out a demonic spirit in a man, and they were rebelliously attacked by that demon, for the reason that they were posing to be men of God but were filled with sin. These same situations however; occur to this present day and are more recognized through forms of witchcraft, voodoo, etc. to which these same fallen angels or demonic spirits, gain full access to use their powers more effectively.

Chapter 3 – The Fall of Lucifer (Satan)

"Thou hast been in Eden the garden of God; every precious stone was thy covering, the sardius, topaz, and the diamond, the beryl, the onyx, and the jasper, the sapphire, the emerald, and the carbuncle, and gold: the workmanship of thy tabrets and of thy pipes was prepared in thee in the day that thou wast created.

Thou *art* the anointed cherub that covereth; and I have set thee *so*: thou wast upon the holy mountain of God; thou hast walked up and down in the midst of the stones of fire.

Thou *wast* perfect in thy ways from the day that thou wast created, till iniquity was found in thee.

By the multitude of thy merchandise they have filled the midst of thee with violence, and thou hast sinned: therefore I will cast thee as profane out of the mountain of God: and I will destroy thee, O covering cherub, from the midst of the stones of fire.

Thine heart was lifted up because of thy beauty, thou hast corrupted thy wisdom by reason of thy brightness: I will cast thee to the ground, I will lay thee before kings, that they may behold thee. Thou hast defiled thy sanctuaries by the multitude

of thine iniquities, by the iniquity of thy traffic; therefore will I bring forth a fire from the midst of thee, it shall devour thee, and I will bring thee to ashes upon the earth in the sight of all them that behold thee. All they that know thee among the people shall be astonished at thee: thou shalt be a terror, and never shalt thou be any more."

Ezekiel 28:13-19

Lucifer, who is now known as "Satan" or "the Devil", was once known as "the anointed cherub". He, in the above passage, was shown to have a special ability that was only given by God and made him stand out from everything else around him. With this anointing, he also was created with infinite beauty, wisdom, and magnitude. His position and the way that God had created him, was unlike to any other cherubim or angel for that matter. He was given the gift of music to which he made a unique sound unto God, that no other angel created was able to make; and being made to perfection, he was also given the individual privilege to cover the presence of God.

This would bring you to assume that he *was* the highest angel created, although it is not mentioned Biblically; he was the cherub that covered God and since he was always in Gods' presence, this caused him to have a great deal of power and authority.

Now that we have discovered who Satan really was, we will take a closer look into what we believe was going on before he was thrown down from the Kingdom of Heaven; but first, we would like to explore for a moment, what may have been the key motivating factor behind God creating man.

Doing research on the human mind, the way that we think, the way we apply ourselves to do things, and what drives us to create, shows evidence that in order to create something, one must first be motivated. Take for instance a man who commits a crime, whether the crime be theft, murder or any other type of vagabond offense, he must first be motivated by something to create such an act. Whether his motivation comes from the lack of money, food, or any type of substance in which this individual requires, he has now become **self motivated** to obtain that specific item by any means necessary.

Another example would be to look into the life of a successful business man who has obtained property, made quality investments, etc. and may live in a mansion by a lake. Although he came from one of the most poverty stricken neighborhoods there is, and his family had nothing much, which resulted in him growing up without the essential needs; yet now, he would be considered a prominent success in life according to his achievements. So grasping onto his background, you would then see where self motivation from this lack, played a key factor at this point.

Because we are made in the image and after the likeness of God; likeness to say, that we *also* do things similar to Him. This shows that in order for God to create man, He in essence, would have had to been motivated. Now the question is: what motivated God?

Let us now go back to that time and envision those events, while reading the scripture below, but a bit more closely.

"How art thou fallen from heaven, O Lucifer, son of the morning! *how* **art thou cut down to the ground, which didst weaken the nations! For thou hast said in thine heart, I will ascend into heaven, I will exalt my throne above the stars of God: I will sit also upon the mount of the congregation, in the sides of the north: I will ascend above the heights of the clouds; I will be <u>like</u> the most High. Yet thou shalt be brought down to hell, to the sides of the pit."**

Isaiah 14:12-15

We know that Lucifer was a very distinct cherubim and he held one of the highest ranked positions.

Although he is now of an evil nature, he at times has been misunderstood, and that is because many don't realize that he was "in fact" not created as an evil spirit; this simply is because God alone created Lucifer, and there is no evil (sin) in Him.

"This then is the message we have heard of Him, and declare unto you, that God is light, and in Him is no darkness at all."

1 John 1:5

This scripture gives reference to show that Lucifer (now Satan) was made without sin and this makes it clearer to see that his rebellion was brought on by choice and *not* from him being originally of a sinful state. We eventually come to see that, even though he was given this distinguished position, somehow, this was not enough to satisfy his interest. By his unique beauty, he became self-absorbed. All of this gradually brought on the spirit of jealousy within Lucifer, but in a completely different aspect.

He no longer saw God as a loving Creator, all he saw now was that God was in charge of **him**. Hence, malicious acts were rooted into his heart and all of this propelled him to act pretentious towards God, and it became evident that his spirit had been turned against God. Being that prized creation in the Kingdom of Heaven was no longer sufficient, he now wanted to *become* the Creator.

The 1/3 of angels that had been cast down along with Satan, were in fact his followers. See the scripture showing this evidence below.

"And his tail drew the third part of the stars in heaven, and did cast them to the earth:"
Revelation 12:4

Satan had somehow managed to lure these angels into believing his way by means of deception; and with that, he caused them to follow and obey *his* every command instead of the commands of *God*. This caused their rebellion towards God, who then cast Lucifer and these angels down from the Kingdom of Heaven to earth, as a place of **imprisonment** for their sinful acts.

CHAPTER 4 – THE CREATION

"In the beginning, God created the Heaven and the earth. And the earth was without form; and void; and darkness was upon the face of the deep."
Genesis 1:1-2

What exactly comes to your mind when you think of the word form, void and darkness? Let us look at this from an exploratory point of view.

When we thought of the word "form", (e.g. "the earth was without **form**", Genesis 1:2) we like many, assumed that it meant specifically the actual shape of the earth. This gave us the impression that the earth was not just round and that it had no specific shape to it at that time; but it was more or less just matter (anything that has weight and takes up space). However; as we grew (in the wisdom of God) over the years, we continued to try and unravel this mystery, and how it came to be.

We then thought about the word "void". Like many of you, we were still under the assumption that it meant emptiness or nothing. But then later as we went on to read again, we came to the word "darkness" as it is stated in the Bible:-

"And darkness was upon the face of the deep."
Genesis 1:2

This began to cause a bit of conflict because we were thinking at first that, if the earth was:

- ❖ without any form
- ❖ It did not contain anything (making it void)
- ❖ And darkness was upon the face of the deep ("deep" meaning water),

What exactly was this scripture trying to say? Let us examine these words **more** closely.

The word "**form**" and the way that it is used in this sentence "and the earth was **without** form", does not in any way mean shape or any type of formation. It simply means "a specific manner in which something was done."

There are many different definitions for one word, however; we must take into consideration that some words depending on the way it is used in context, can have a very *specific* definition to it. So we realized now, that you must place the *correct* definition within a sentence according to what is being stated.

We then examined the word "**void**" and the way it is used in this continued sentence "and the earth was without form; and **void**." When it states void, it meant specifically for the aspect in which it was being referred to, which was "not legally binding, no given order or no law."

Lastly, the word "**darkness**" as it is used also in this sentence "and **darkness** was upon the face of the deep." Darkness in this sentence is not referred to as a state in which there is no visual light; but instead it meant more specifically "wickedness or evil."

Now that we have presented these scriptures and gathered the correct meanings to those words given; we will now re-read this passage and replace those words highlighted above, with the meanings given. This will cause us to gain **full** understanding to what it was meant to be, in its original format.

"In the beginning, God created the heaven and the earth. And the earth was without **a specific manner in which something was done** and **not legally binding, with no given order and no law;** and **wickedness/evil** was upon the face of the waters."

Genesis 1:1-2

We believe that this scripture is now presented in complete fullness, and it has given total revelation to where the *truth* can now be understood. In regards to those previous doctrines that we were once taught concerning this matter, this not only brought us into confusion, but it also gave to a way of deception. Why deception? This is because when most people have read this scripture, they may have "in fact" been either uncertain on some of the aspects of this scripture, or they would not challenge some of those theologians providing what was said to be; simply because it was established this *way* for centuries. Therefore; some people will more than likely avoid any possible conflict from asking this question or showing disbelief due to what it may have caused.

"And the earth was without form, and void; and darkness was upon the face of the deep. And the Spirit of God moved upon the face of the waters. **And God said, Let there be light: and there was light. And God saw the light. That *it was* good. and God divided the light from the darkness.**"

Genesis 1:2-4

The first thing that you need to understand in reference to this scripture is, when God said "Let there be light." What exactly *did* He mean by "light"? Did He mean the brightness of the sky? Most of us would possibly think first that He did mean this, and then again some of you may say, did He mean something else? Our personal opinion on this is that He *did* mean something else.

If you remember the darkness that the Spirit hovered over, it was not actually darkness meaning the absence of light, but this darkness was in regards to the evil and wickedness that was present on the earth. When God said "Let there be light" He did not mean the light as in brightness; He instead was referring to specifically, one of the many meanings of light. This as it is defined from The New American Webster Handy College Dictionary Third Edition was to be "**Principles of conduct**" or in other words a way in which things operate, or to place things in a particular order.

Now you might be saying to yourself, how did you come to this conclusion?" We clarify this by showing you three (3) key points:

1. We have already established the fact that Lucifer had been abolished from the Kingdom of Heaven/God. (Isaiah 14:12 and Luke 10:18.) More specifically, he was cast down to the earth. This explains why there was darkness and wickedness present on earth. Therefore; since the earth had no form, which we discovered meant "a specific manner in which something was done" and was void which means "without given order or no law". We have now come to know that in an evil atmosphere with no order and no law to where wickedness *can* rule and reign, this would be such a setting for God, who is a God of decency and order (1 Corinthians 14:40) to come in and establish principles

of conduct; or in other words "Let there be light."

2. **"And God saw the light, that *it was* good: and God divided the light from the darkness. And God called the light Day, and the darkness He called Night. And the evening and the morning were the first day."**

Genesis 1:4-5

Now that we have already established that the light represented the principles of conduct and that the darkness represented evil. We must look to why God called the light day, and the darkness He called night. In no sense, was this meant to be only that of the daytime or the nighttime in that aspect. God knew that he had to separate the light from the darkness, that being Day and Night. He also had to establish a way in which they would be separated completely from each other.

We know that evil does not have principles of conduct and this is simply because it does whatever it wants, whenever it feels like doing so in a *self*-righteous manner. These two forms presented here, though it may seem slightly confusing, were "in fact" being placed within its proper environment. Take for example, during the day in which light operates, you would have more people who are willing to conduct themselves in an orderly manner; whereas during nighttime in which evil thrives at the most, you would then have *less* people who are willing to act in the previous manner because it is much more difficult to detect when something will bring about a problem and when it will occur as versus to the daytime. Therefore; the Day represented as the light, is of order and moral, and the Night represented as the darkness is of less light, which can bring about displeasing and unsuitable situations. This gives clarity to show exactly why light and darkness can not co-exist at the same given time.

3. **"And God said, Let there be lights in the firmament of the heaven to divide the day from the night; and let them be for signs, and for seasons, and for days, and years: And let them be for lights in the firmament of the heaven to give light upon the earth: and it was so. And God made two great lights; the greater light to rule the day, and the lesser light to rule the night; He made the stars also. And God set them in the firmament of the heaven to give light upon the earth, And to rule over the day and over the night, and to divide the light from the darkness: and God saw that it was good. And the evening and the morning were the fourth day."**

Genesis 1:14-19

The scripture shown has caused many including ourselves in the past, to become very confused. Some would say that these two scriptures Genesis 1:3-4 and Genesis 1:14-19 bring contradiction to itself. For this reason, some may assume that in verses 3 through 4, when God created the light, that there *was* physical light, However; it then shows further along into the scripture where He placed lights in the sky (e.g. sun, moon & stars.) in verses 14 through 19. So this would bring you to ask, how exactly was the day and night functioning if there were no sun, moon and stars present on the first day instead of four days later? Were light, being the Day, and darkness being the Night, still functioning without the actual physical light that we see with our eyes?

We must remember that in the beginning, God said "Let there be **light**." He never said let there be a sun or moon to give light to the earth. So we must now take into consideration that the light that God first spoke into existence was not the visual light that we now perceive with the eyes. This was a principle that was spoken into existence in order to establish a specific way of doing things.

If you noticed after each day as continued from verse 3 onward; before it is mentioned "And evening and morning were the first, second, third, fourth, etc. day". This was because we were now beginning to see God's specific order in the way things were being created. This in itself shows that everything must have principles of conduct or a specific manner in which things are done. For example, the sun rises in the morning without the moon. The sun will always rise in the sky as long as it is aligned in its' proper setting and never otherwise. Just as we human beings awake from our sleep; otherwise we know that if we don't awake in "normal" circumstances, we are no longer alive and the spiritual laws that God applied to us here on earth, would no longer be in effect; hence you have succumb to the aspect of death.

Therefore, when we look at verses 14 through 19, when the sun, moon and stars were being created; it was *now* a physical light that was being brought into manifestation. This gives solid evidence to prove the separation of the two lights shown in scripture; the first was related to the spiritual aspect, and the next was related to the aspect of (physical) sun or moon light. In the beginning God had to *first* establish those spiritual laws that would govern the earth before He could move forward in creating the physical atmosphere that we dwell in today.

The creation of man

"What is man, that Thou art mindful of him? And the Son of man, that Thou visitest him? For Thou has made him a little lower than the angels, and has crowned him with glory and honour. Thou madest him to have dominion over the works of Thy hands; Thou has put all things under his feet."

Psalm 8:4-6

We begin by asking the question, why did God create man? This now brings us to focus again on what was the key motivating factor for God to create man (as mentioned briefly, earlier in chapter 3) and His ultimate purpose for us here on earth?

"And God said, Let us make man in our image, after our likeness: and let them have dominion over the fish of the sea, and over the fowl of the air, and over the cattle, and over all the earth, and over every creeping thing that creepeth upon the earth. So God created man in His own image, in the image of God created He him; male and female created He them. And God blessed them, and God said unto them, Be fruitful, and multiply, and replenish the earth, and subdue it: and have dominion over the fish

of the sea, and over the fowl of the air, and over every living thing that moveth upon the earth."

Genesis 1:26-28

"And the LORD God formed man *of* the dust of the ground, and breathed into his nostrils the breath of life; and **man became a living soul**."

Genesis 2:7

We must first look into the mind of God, whilst recapping the key point to His motivation; which gradually brought Him to create a being that was **"a little lower than the angels"** and gave to him dominion over the entire earth. This is where we need you (the reader) to now visualize the following scene for a moment.

Imagine Lucifer the Chief cherubim in the Kingdom of Heaven, placed in a position next to God; and because of this privilege, he is given the authority to give charge over God's army of angels. Anything that was needed to be done went through him. Basically here, we are saying that he was the Vice President of the Kingdom of Heaven. However; like some Vice Presidents', they may eventually come to develop a great deal of envy and jealousy; whereas these emotions now play a major part in their agendas. Instead of them taking and giving those orders as directed to do so, they would rather be the ones' in **full** control. This too was the position that Lucifer had, but *he* was the one from which this behavior originated.

So since God is the President, and He noticed the change in behavior within Lucifer; He finally decided to banish Lucifer and his followers from the Kingdom of Heaven, by casting them to the earth which was set as a place of imprisonment for them. There was no order or no laws in place at that given time; but as time progressed, Satan and his followers who represented this darkness, more than likely began to rebel again by doing even more disorderly and detest things that would soon eventually stir up the anger and wrath within God. God who is *the* God, who alone reigns and rules over all; devised the ultimate plan to destroy Satan's continuous rebellion towards Him. This is where the Creation of man is introduced.

Now, we would like you take a moment to just stop and think about the scripture shown here. Genesis 1:26 states "And God said, Let us make man in our image, after our likeness" If we carefully review the statement that was made here, it actually sounds as if man was *already* in existence. Let us examine this more closely.

"And God said <u>Let us</u> (the Holy Trinity) make (the state that he is now presented in and cause him) man (to be conformed) in *our* image, after *our* likeness."

We must also take into consideration that Satan's powers are very much in effect to this present day. See the scripture as referenced to this matter.

"And no marvel (wonderful act)**; for Satan himself is transformed into an angel of light."**
2 Corinthians 11:14

This verifies that God did not strip him of his powers after he was cast down from the Kingdom of Heaven. Therefore; would it be insane to think that Satan, whilst on this earth in his state of imprisonment, went ahead and began to create something that was labeled as "man"? Would it even be impossible to believe that he *was* "in fact" trying to create man to have the external image/shape of what he saw God as before he was banished from Gods' Kingdom? With that, was he making this alleged image to be similar to God's own image (as a means of spite) to perhaps bow down and worship *him* as if he were God. In essence, God already had angels that worshipped Him without end, therefore; it would only justify why Satan would want to receive that same worship from his own creation.

For thou hast said in thine heart, I will ascend into heaven, I will exalt my throne above the stars of God: I will sit also upon the mount of the congregation, in the sides of the north: I will ascend above the heights of the clouds; I will be <u>like</u> the most High.

                                                    Isaiah 14:13-14

After taking all of this into consideration, one might strongly oppose to what is being said here, because it would then make God seem as a fraud to what most of us know Him as, which is "The Creator". However; what you must realize is that God truly *is* "The Creator of all". You might already be saying, how is it possible for us to say this when we have just stated that Satan could have been the original creator for our mankind? Are we posing a contradiction to the beliefs that have been established through His word? With the full assurance from God, we say to you, that this is not the intention.

Momentarily we will see how the Word of God comes to reveal this. With all verses given in Genesis chapter 1, God is shown to be the start in which all things were created. In each of the following verses, pay close attention to the way things were brought into existence or rather established.

Genesis 1:1 "In the beginning **God created** the heaven and the earth."

Genesis 1:3 "And **God said, Let there be** light: and there was light."

Genesis 1:4 "And **God called** the light Day, and the darkness **He called** Night."

Genesis 1:6 "And **God said, Let there be** a firmament in the midst of the waters, and **let** it divide the waters from the waters."

Genesis 1:7 "And **God made** the firmament, and divided the waters which *were* under the firmament from the waters which *were* above the firmament and it was so."

Genesis 1:8 "And **God called** the firmament Heaven."

Genesis 1:9 "And **God said, Let** the waters under the heaven be gathered together unto one place, and **let** the dry *land* appear: and it was so."

Genesis 1:10 "And **God called** the dry *land* Earth: and the gathering together of the waters **called He** Seas, and God saw that *it was* good."

Genesis 1:11 " And **God said, Let** the earth bring forth grass, the herb yielding seed, *and* the fruit tree yielding fruit seed after his kind, whose seed *is* in itself, upon the earth: and it was so."

Genesis 1:14-15 "And **God said, Let** there be lights in the firmament of heaven to divide the day from the night; and **let** them be for signs, and for seasons, and for days, and years: And **let them be** for lights in the firmament of the heaven to give light upon the earth: and it was so.

Genesis 1:16 "And **God made** two great lights; the greater light to rule the day, and the lesser light to rule the night: *He made* the stars also."

Genesis 1:20 "And **God said, Let** the waters bring forth abundantly the moving creature that hath life, and fowl *that* may fly above the earth in the open firmament of heaven."

Genesis 1:21 "And **God created** great whales, and every living creature that moveth, which the waters brought forth abundantly, after their kind, and every winged fowl after his kind: and God saw that *it was* good.

Genesis 1:24 "And **God said, Let** the earth bring forth the living creature after his kind, cattle, and creeping thing, and beast of the earth after his kind: and it was so."

Genesis 1:25 "And **God made** the beast of the earth after his kind, and cattle after their kind, and everything that creepeth upon the earth after his kind: and God saw that *it was* good."

Now that we have seen that everything that was first spoken into existence and then established by God, resulted in Him speaking them into existence in a specific manner. Whether it stated "God created", "God said Let there be", "God called" and "God made"; all of these correspond to give proof that the things created **originally** by God were always worded in this manner.

However; when we go on to read about the creation of man, the order in which He spoke the creation of things was reversed.

"And God said, **Let us <u>make man in our</u> image**, after our likeness...So **God created man in <u>His</u>**

__*own*__ **image**, in the image of God created He him; male and female created He them."

Genesis 1:26 & 27

This now presents the challenge of why did God say "let us make man" rather than, **then God made man** or **God created man to be in His own image, after His likeness,** first? Did he already have a patent that was made with merely some of the similarities to Himself? And if this man was made as such, was he re-creating this man specifically in His exact image and after *His* own likeness, to where now there was no mistake to be made in this manner? Would it be strange to even imagine that this form of man *was* given the ability to live but instead; God, decided to redesign the man in His own image and after His own likeness, and gave him the very essence of God, which is, that this man was now able to possess a soul that was his own.

We believe the scriptures mentioned earlier and the two that will be specified to follow below; will "in fact" bring great depth to this revelation. Therefore; we now present to you as possibly "new evidence" that may cause the original theory on the creation of man, to now be looked on as otherwise.

In Psalm 51:5 it states **"Behold, I was shapen in iniquity, and in sin did my mother conceive me."**

Before we move forward with this, take a brief moment to interpret first from "your own" understanding as to what this scripture means in your point of view.

We will now begin to explore the revelation behind what this scripture truly means. When we see the word "shapen" or rather shaped, we must first come to understand exactly what this word means before we can receive the true revelation from this scripture.

While reading, we often have a tendency to skip pass words that we think we already understand, because we have become too engulfed in what is about to take place. When we do this, our intake of understanding is minimized; this shows the importance as to why we should study those specific words instead of just reading past them. Once we begin to do so, we will be able to fully comprehend that which is being said. So now we will move on to explore these words from that scripture and look at other possible meanings that they may reveal, instead of that from a common belief.

❖ **Shaped** – an imaginary form; phantom.
❖ **Iniquity** – wickedness
❖ **Sin** – originated from Satan, therefore sin is represented by Satan.
❖ **Conceive** - to form a notion or idea of; imagine.
❖ **Mother** - To be the mother of; give origin or rise to. (In this case, that would be from which the conception of man took place.)

Now we will replace these words that are shown in Psalms 51:5 with the definitions given above.

"Behold, I was shapen in iniquity" – Behold I was **imagined** in **wickedness**, "and in sin did my mother conceive me"– and in **sin** *did* **Satan** form a notion or an idea of me (man).

So in other words, Satan who is sin and the conception of man being created in sin, would in essence show that we were conceived in the mind of Satan, and gives more clarity to how man came to be.

Now that we have taken into consideration the depths of what this scripture has revealed, one can only begin to imagine how this original form of man actually was. Now you may ask, could this be possible enough, to be the starting point from which the Caveman Age begun?

Instead of thinking back to times of when apes originated and believing that this was where we began, we more or less had our origination brought in to manifestation by means of an attempt to replicate the image of God; but only in the worst way possible.

When you begin to picture the state in which these men were made, this alone could give plausible reason to the bowing posture that we have come to understand these prehistoric men once had. However; because they were under a controlled mindset and lacked the very essence of what God gave to his re-creation of man, which was a soul that possessed a unique purpose in itself; Cavemen instead lacked the intelligence that is required to become fully functional.

Looking at the first commandment in full depth and what is being said; it truly gives more evidence as to why this could and even may be true.

"And God spake all these words, saying, I am the LORD thy God, which have brought thee out of the land of Egypt, out of the house of bondage. Thou shalt have no other gods before me. Thou

shalt not make unto thee (thyself) any graven image, or any likeness of any thing that is in heaven above, or that is in the earth beneath, or that is in the water under the earth: Thou shalt not bow down thyself to them, nor serve them: For I the LORD thy God am a jealous God."

Exodus 20:1-5

We must once again mention to those of you who are not familiar with the Bible and its passages; that this particular verse does not end just as such. Once you continue to read onward, you will see why God says these things and inevitably what the outcome will result in depending on whether you choose to or choose not to follow His commands.

However; we have purposely ended the scripture at this point to show the clarity and that there were specifications made. God made it clear enough to us, by letting us know that He is God alone and there is none like Him. He also forbids you to create for yourselves graven images to bow down to and that man should not create them regardless of whence they came; whether it be either in Heaven, (from where the first graven image was taken) on earth and under the earth and in the sea beneath. After all of this is stated God finally tells you **why** you are not to do this.

Because He *truly* is a jealous God and **will not** tolerate His position being shared, He makes it known to **all,** well in advance if you decided to show interests in making such images (Isaiah 46:9 & 2 Corinthians 10:5).

To conclude this point and the truth that we firmly believe it holds, we have based on the simple fact of how each of Gods' signature creations were indicated. The scriptures in regards to those things created by God are stated with at the end of its verse, "And God saw that *it was* **good.**" However; when it comes to the creation of man, that statement was rather left unsaid. This was because we were not originally Gods' creation; after God had completely re-designed us to have the full capacity to live, think and have much similarities to Him, we were received to be (literally) "blessed" after this.

In other words because God is good and this is only what He represents, **everything** that originated from Him alone, had to follow in that very same manner. However; when we think of Satan, we already know that he *is* filled with wickedness and only has that of a sinful nature; anything that originated from him could only be of *that* very same manner, and that would be wicked and sinful.

So now you may ask, how could it be that we, Gods' most esteemed creature, who was given the greatest command since creation which was to have **dominion** over <u>all</u>, to be **fruitful** and to **multiply** and to **replenish** this earth whilst **subduing** it, *not* be something that was good indeed? It really gives you something to consider, and if we are correct, *that* would only be because we weren't originally created by God, but instead our original format was by that of Satan; and there truly is not *anything* **"good"** about that.

We believe that this revelation was given to us by the grace of God and that is through the Holy Spirit. Although it may seem to be a strange theory and it may not be pleasing to some, whether you have decided to believe this or not; this in our belief, shows that this was originally how the creation of man must have come to be.

Remember, you do not have to teach a child how to do wrong because this sinful state comes to them naturally; but we must always teach them how to do right, which "in fact" does not come to us **naturally**.

CHAPTER 5 – THE FALL OF MAN

When we look at the fall of man, in order to understand the full consequence of man's disobedience towards God, we must first gain an understanding of how Satan was connected to this fall.

Earth before its transformation, was in a state that we believe was the ideal environment for Satan and his followers to be imprisoned. We assume now that since God came to put an end to what was taking place, He decided to put order into effect which then caused the state of Satan's environment to be changed; and because of this, the level of Satan's animosity was increased to a point where he became infuriated.

Now we can begin to see the relevance in why Satan devised a plan that should have made evil thrive eternally, as he originally anticipated it would have remained, before God decided to make His unannounced appearance and permanently change those possibilities. We ask that you would please pay close attention to what you are about to read.

Most people are very familiar with this story:

God created man and gave him dominion over everything. He then created a woman that was taken from the rib of this man, and God later tells the man that they can eat from any tree in the garden, except for one particular tree. Man eventually comes into disobedience to God by eating from this tree *with* his wife, therefore; they are now removed from the Garden of Eden. Some time later the woman who is now known as Eve has two sons who are called Cain and Abel. Cain however; killed his brother, and from this point on, the civilization of man begun to emerge.

Now this story in particular is one that we often hear in different parts of the world that share some of our religious beliefs. Let us now retrace those events and investigate them more carefully.

In order for us to establish the truths within this chapter, more specifically Genesis chapter 3; we must first ask these questions:

1. How did Eve come to speak with the serpent?
2. What was the tree of knowledge of good and evil; and what exactly was its' fruit?
3. Why was this tree placed in the garden if God did not want Adam and Eve to go near to its' presence?
4. Why did Adam disregard Gods' command?
5. What was the tree of life?

These questions will help us to better comprehend and grasp onto the missing but most intricate parts of the creation story that is *too* often misunderstood.

Question 1. How did Eve come to speak with the serpent?

Now most of us already know that God gave Adam a woman to be a help meet unto him, but at the same time we also know that Satan was lurking and waiting for the right opportunity to retrieve what he felt was taken from him. So let us visualize Adam and Eve gathering berries and then Eve steps away for a brief moment.

We have to bear in mind that if a man is interested in a woman who is always with her mate, that man will have to wait for a precise moment when she is out of her mate's presence, where he can then present himself to her. This is what we believe Satan did.
Satan always knew that Eve was there with Adam and that she was to be a help meet unto him; so what better way to get to Adam but through someone whom he loved, trusted and shared his throne with; and the reason we say "throne" specifically, is because Adam was positioned by God to be a king in the garden and for that reason, he ruled over everything that was in it.

Satan, being a spirit who was very much aware of Adams consistent presence with Eve, realized that since they often spoke with the animals together, this presented a **doorway** for him to communicate with them, and that occurred when Eve was alone. Had anyone of these animals approached Eve under normal circumstances whereby reason of their size and height, Adam would take notice of this and therefore be able to intervene. However; for the reason that the serpent was a more subtle creature, that was very sly with its approach; when that moment had finally presented itself; Satan used his spirit to possess the serpent that was less visible to notice.

The serpent now went on to say "Yea, hath God said, Ye shall not eat of every tree of the garden? And the woman said unto the serpent, We may eat of the fruit of the trees of the garden: But of the fruit of the tree which is in the midst of the garden, God hath said, Ye shall not eat of it, neither shall ye touch it, lest ye die.
And the Serpent said unto the woman "Ye shall not surely die: For God doth know that in the day ye eat thereof, then your eyes shall be opened, and ye shall be as gods, knowing good and evil."

Genesis 3:1-5

We now understand the fact that, Satan's job was not just to talk to Eve, but to convince **her** that it *was* okay to go by the tree of knowledge of good and evil and to eat of its fruit; because he knew that once he had persuaded her she would then persuade her husband.

If you pay close attention to what the scripture says, you will see where it distinguishes in **Genesis 3:1-4** that she *was* "in fact" alone at first, because the dialogue is continuously shown where only she and the serpent are discussing what Adam had been told about the tree by God; and since her husband did not even realize that this conversation was taking place; it makes it easier to see that he was not present because it never shows where he participated in this conversation.

We must also consider the fact that had Adam been there at first, he more than likely would've intervened after hearing what the serpent had said to Eve. But seeing that he wasn't there and he now saw her move over to the tree of knowledge of good and evil on her own, where they had been forbidden to go; he then followed to see why she suddenly wanted to be in its presence.

"And when the woman saw that the tree *was* good for food, and that it *was* pleasant to the eyes, and a tree to be desired to make *one* wise, **she** took of the fruit thereof, and did eat, and gave also unto her husband **with her**, and he did eat."

Genesis 3:6

Now that we have established why Eve took of this fruit from the tree of knowledge of good and evil, this now brings us to our second question:

Question 2. What was the tree of knowledge of good and evil; and what exactly was its' fruit?

If we take into account how the dialogue between Eve and the serpent is brought across and what God had said prior to this, about all the trees in the garden that they could eat; when regarding the tree that they were forbidden to eat from, more specifically He stated "the tree of **knowledge of** good and evil". In order for something to have knowledge *of* something else it must first have a life force.

For example, a chair does not know that its' a chair, it does not make conversation with other chairs and it holds no secrets. In order for God to make such a bold statement and say that something knows good and evil, clearly states that this is not an ordinary tree; because if it really was an ordinary tree the statement would have been changed to "the tree **of** good and evil". Therefore this tree had to possess a knowledgeable spirit.

We have been taught specifically that during that time, the only "beings" present in the garden was Adam and Eve, the animals (among them was the serpent) and the Spirit of God. Yet what we may have neglected to realize for many years now is that the spirit of Satan was also among them.

How do we know that Satan was present? If you remember earlier when we mentioned that he possessed the serpent, you have to first understand why he had to do this. Satan was the tree of knowledge of good and evil, therefore; it was **not** a physical tree that we assumed it to be. Instead it *was* a spirit in the midst of the garden and this is why God referred to him as "the tree of knowledge of good and evil." Scripture reference of this is shown below:

"<u>Thou hast been in</u> **Eden the garden of God; every precious stone was thy covering**, the sardius, topaz, and the diamond, the beryl, the onyx, and the jasper, the sapphire, the emerald, and the carbuncle, and gold: the workmanship of thy tabrets and of thy pipes was prepared in thee in the day that thou wast created.

Thine heart was lifted up because of thy beauty, thou <u>hast corrupted</u> **thy wisdom by reason of thy brightness** (brightness meaning intelligence; filled with knowledge): **I will cast thee to the ground,**"

Ezekiel 28:13 &17

Now that we have clarity of what is being said here, we must also regard the fact that though Satan was in the garden, he was very much aware of the command that was given to Adam and Eve. Therefore; because he was not able to be in two or more places at the same time (as God *is* omnipresent); he could only cause his spirit to possess the serpent at first, who would then persuade Eve and cause her to move over to that area where he would be positioned *again*.

Given that we have established both of these points we fully understand what the tree was in this garden. We know that this tree who was Satan, still obtained the original powers and appearance for the reason that the scripture (above) never mentioned that God removed his powers and beauty from him. This is why Eve was so fascinated and completely absorbed by what she had just seen. See as shown below:

" And when the woman **saw** that the tree *was* good for food, and that it *was* **pleasant to the eyes**, and a tree to be **desired** to make *one* wise,"

Genesis 3:6

This now brings us to the second part of this question and that is: **what exactly was this fruit?**

Seeing that we have a substantial amount of evidence as to why this was not an actual tree; this brings us to the fruit of this same tree and how we have come to realize that this too could not be an actual fruit. So in order to distinguish what it is we must first perceive this from a spiritual point of view.

The scripture states in Genesis 2:17 "**in the day that thou eatest thereof thou shalt surely die.**" In order for someone to eat something, one must first intake of it. Because we are looking at this from a spiritual point of view, we must also know what spiritual food truly is.

Spiritual food is a resource of information that is given to strengthen the spirit man of an individual in specific areas. For example Proverbs 18:20-21 states "**A man's belly shall be satisfied with the <u>fruit</u> of his mouth**; (by the words that he says) ***and*** **with the increase of his lips shall he be filled. Death and life** ***are*** **in the power of the tongue: and they that love it shall** ***eat*** **the <u>fruit</u> thereof.**"(For example, they that love *death* specifically shall eat the fruit yielded from it; which means that things such as pain, hatred, depression, etc. will become manifested in that individuals' life.)

We are now able to see that when Eve ate of the fruit and gave then also to Adam; they both took in or received the things that were being spoken to them; because immediately thereafter their eyes were opened. This only came to be through their belief in what was being said to them by Satan, and instead they rejected the command that God had spoken to Adam (that was applied to them both).

To finalize this belief, you must read Genesis 3:9-11 that is shown below:

"And the Lord God called unto Adam, and said unto him, Where art thou? And he said, I heard thy voice in the garden, and I was afraid, because I was naked; and I hid myself. And He said, **Who** told thee that thou *wast* naked? Hast thou **eaten of the tree**, whereof I commanded thee that thou shouldest not eat?"

Clarity is given here by means of God associating the tree with a **who** instead of a **what**; and by doing so, if one uses the term "who" it would refer to someone likewise if one uses the term "what" it would refer to a thing. Overall, because God had associated the tree with a "who" this justified that it had to be someone which implies that this was either a "being" or a "spirit".

Question 3. Why was this tree placed in the garden if God did not want Adam and Eve to go near to its' presence?

Because we have come to establish that the tree of knowledge of good and evil was none other than Satan, we believe that God placed him in the midst of the garden as a part of his punishment. God did this because Satan had tried to create a form of man to bow down and worship him, so that he would feel as though *he was* God. However, through God being all knowing and having seen this iniquity in the heart of Satan, God then brought forth a vengeance suitable for his vigorous efforts made by this continuously sinful manner.

"Vengeance *belongeth* unto me, I will recompense, saith the Lord."

Hebrews 10:30

Therefore; when God placed him in the midst of the garden, he took what Satan had made and re-created it to be in *His* own image and after His likeness, and gave dominion and authority to rule over all things, **<u>especially</u>** Satan himself. This only reinforced to Satan, that God *is* the only One and true living God and no one will ever take out of His possession who He is, and that is Alpha and Omega, The Beginning and The End.

"For I *am* God, and *there is* none else; *I am* God, and *there is* none like me."

Isaiah 46:9

"Thou shalt not bow down thyself to them, nor serve them: For I the LORD thy God *am* a jealous God."
Exodus 20:5

Question 4. Why did Adam disregard Gods' command?

First of all, we believe beyond all that had occurred that Adam did not purposely intend to disobey Gods' command. However; we feel as though there may have been a lot of things going on in his mind such as having a wife who was supportive and at that, one who may have wanted her husband to yield to her interests also. He may have also thought that if he didn't compromise with her to some degree; he would have appeared to be showing neglect towards her feelings.

If you look at the modern man for example, and the relationship between male and female, once we (couples) are considered to be "in love", a man will go to *any* extent to please that woman. So we must place ourselves in Adams' position and know that when Adam made the statement **"This is now bone of my bones, and flesh of my flesh"** he proclaims in other words, that this woman is like the spinal cord to the body, without it the body is not able to function making it useless. So this shows the measure of extent to what a man would do for a woman that he truly loves.

The evidence that is shown in regards to this belief is when God was about to deal with the sin that they became involved in, God's punishment *specifically* to the woman was one of "great" affliction. Genesis 3:16 states "Unto the woman He said, I will **greatly** multiply thy sorrow and thy conception; in sorrow thou shalt bring forth children; and **thy desire *shall be* to thy husband**, and **he shall rule over thee**." In essence God made certain that Adams desire would no longer be unto that of his wife but now, her desire would be unto *him* and with that "*He* shall rule over her" and no longer the reverse.

So if you find yourself still asking, *why did* Adam disregard Gods' command? Place yourself in his shoes for a moment and then ask yourself would *you* have done it any differently?

Question 5. What was the tree of life?

The tree of life is first mentioned in Genesis 2:9 where it states **"And out of the ground made the LORD God to grow every tree that is pleasant to the sight, and good for food; <u>the tree of life</u> also in the midst of the garden, and the tree of knowledge of good and evil."**

We must understand that this tree was also not like any other physical tree that we see. This tree was spiritual but with that it gave a special presence to the Garden of Eden because it shared in the embodiment of the Holy Trinity; in other words this tree was the spirit of Jesus Christ.

This may seem to be a very bold statement to suggest, but once you have come to the realization that Gods' Son (Jesus) partakes in the way of life, it will become of a great insight.

Let us explore these scriptures that give relevance to what is being said here.

In John 3:16 which some of us are familiar with, this scripture gives the answer to what many have searched and still seek to know even up to this present day, and that is "what will happen after this life has passed from us?" This scripture gives us with full assurance and beyond all doubt that the True Redeemer, once received into our lives, *will* from that moment on, never leave us nor forsake us (Hebrews 13:5-6) and gives to them the assurance that we *will* have an eternal destiny with God.

"For God so loved the world, that He gave His only begotten Son, that whosoever believeth in Him should not perish, but have everlasting life."

John 3:16

The Son of God that is mentioned in this scripture is Jesus Christ; however this scripture was given during the time when Jesus came from the spiritual realm and was made manifest through the flesh of the Virgin Mary, Jesus' mother. Because of His gift of self-sacrifice for our (mankind's) sins, we through Him are able to be reconnected with our Father in the Kingdom of Heaven.

To bring clarity to where He is linked to the tree of life, it is revealed through the following scriptures:

"Jesus saith unto him, I am the way, the truth and the **life**; no man cometh unto the Father, <u>but by me.</u>"

John 14:6

If we examine this in more depth, it is revealed in Revelation 22:2 as it states "In the midst of the street of it, and on either side of the river, *was there* the **tree of life**, which bare twelve *manner* of fruits (the 12 tribes of Israel), *and* yielded her fruit every month: and the leaves of the tree *were* the healing of the nations."

We can also cross reference "**the healing of the nations**" as mentioned in this scripture with that in **Isaiah 53:5**, which was a prophetic message that was given to show the afflictions that the future

Messiah (Jesus) would bare on behalf of our sins; thus bringing healing, deliverance, and new life to all who received it.

"Blessed *are* they that do His commandments, that they may have right to the tree of life, and may enter in through the gates into the city."
Revelation 22:14

All these scriptures coincide and connect to reveal the glory of the Garden of Eden; which was the tree of life that was the essence, to always project the omnipresence of God.

All of these scriptures are sealed through the assurance by what God had spoken within the Holy Trinity after Adam and Eve had received the curse of sin, (evil nature) which is shown in Genesis 3:22. It brings forth the evidence needed to link all these scriptures presented.

"And the LORD God said, Behold, the man is become as one of **us**, to know good and evil: and now, lest he put forth his hand and take also of the **tree of life** and eat, and live forever."

Now that we have established who Jesus is within the Holy Trinity; we know that before His physical manifestation was brought forth to the earth; He remained Spirit prior to this event. However; because we know that He *is* the way to eternal life, it would only be rational to see why God stated what He did in the scripture above.

For Adam and Eve to have received from this tree, the gift of eternal life and with that knowing that *only* Jesus was The One who could give man the redemption needed in order to acquire this eternal promise; it then brings you to wonder and even see as plausible, that God had for them to be removed due to the fact that Satan's idea (as mentioned earlier in this chapter) of Adam and Eve becoming "as gods" but in a sinful nature; would have only been a plan that was well executed, had they been allowed to become immortal, hence giving evil the right to thrive and live eternally as God.

So now that we know that our Savior (the tree of life) was ever-present before He was presented to man later as The Redeemer; we therefore know that God *had* intended for us to be redeemed after the curse of sin had taken place. This is simply by the reason that the creation of man made over into *His* (Gods') image and after *His* likeness, was far **too great** of a sacrifice to easily loose at any cost. Therefore; He inevitably made it possible for us to experience this privilege again, but after having the chains of sin destroyed from us.

"The Lord is not slack concerning His promise, as some men count slackness; but is longsuffering to us-ward, **not willing that <u>any</u>** should perish, but that **all should come to repentance**."

2 Peter 3:9

Chapter 6 – Coats of Skins

❧

We know that when you see "**coats of skins**" you may begin to ask yourself, what could they possibly be talking about?

As we read the book of Genesis, everything from the tree of knowledge of good and evil, down to the twelve tribes of Israel; we have found that many of us are more or less trained in our mindset by the way in which we read. We would only pay close attention to specific things and tend to neglect some of the most intricate (and sometimes intimidating) details in the book of Genesis. Such as, for example, areas that show why some curses have been brought upon us from the beginning of mankind.

However; when it comes down to this topic, we have heard many men of God make numerous attempts to answer this one particular question, and that is, "what did it mean specifically when God made coats of skins for Adam and Eve, and then clothed them?"

Many have explained what they believed to have happened when Adam and Eve sinned, especially regarded towards the coats of skins. Some have said that because Adam and Eve said that "**they were naked**", God therefore; wanted to cover them as a sign of forgiveness for this sin of disobedience. God then took an animal which was *pure* and *with out* blemish, and sacrificed it back to himself on their behalf. He then took the skin from this animal and made tunics to clothe them. This was done particularly because Adam and Eve had originally covered their bodies with fig leaves. After God had clothed them, He sent them away from the Garden of Eden.

In other words, God took the skin from this animal (which was also unknown) and made leather outfits for them. This is what some people truly believe, but in our opinion this is just not plausible enough.

So go with us for a moment, on a journey that will explore the depths behind this theory of "**coats of skins**".

"And the Lord God caused a deep sleep to fall upon Adam, and he slept: and He took one of his ribs, and closed up the flesh instead thereof; And the rib which the Lord God had taken from man, made He a woman, and brought her unto the man.

And Adam said, This *is* now bone of my bones, and flesh of my flesh: she shall be called Woman, because she was taken out of Man."

Genesis 2:21-23

"And the serpent said unto the woman, Ye shall not surely die: For God doth know that in the day ye eat thereof, then your eyes shall be opened, and ye shall be as gods, knowing good and evil.

And when the woman saw that the tree *was* good for food, and that it was pleasant to the eyes, and a tree to be desired to make one wise, she took of the fruit thereof, and did eat, and gave also unto her husband with her; and he did eat.

And the eyes of them both were opened, and they knew that they were naked; and they sewed fig leaves together, and made themselves aprons.

And they heard the voice of the LORD God walking in the garden in the cool of the day: and Adam and his wife hid themselves from the presence of the LORD God amongst the trees of the garden.

And the LORD God called unto Adam, and said unto him, Where art thou?

And he said, I heard thy voice in the garden, and I was afraid, because I was naked; and I hid myself.

And He said, Who told thee that thou wast naked? Hast thou eaten of the tree, whereof I commanded thee thou shouldest not eat?

And the man said, The woman thou gavest to be with me, she gave me of the tree, and I did eat.

And the LORD God said unto the woman, What is this that thou hast done?' And the woman said, The serpent beguiled me, and I did eat.
And the LORD God said unto the serpent, Because thou hast done this, thou art cursed above all cattle, and above every beast of the field; upon thy belly shalt thou go, and dust shalt thou eat all the days of thy life:

And I will put enmity between thee and the woman, and between thy seed and her seed; it shall bruise thy head, and thou shalt bruise his heel.

Unto the woman He said, I will greatly multiply thy sorrow and thy conception; in sorrow thou shalt bring forth children; and thy desire shall be to thy husband, and he shall rule over thee.

And unto Adam He said, Because thou hast hearkened unto the voice of thy wife, and hast eaten of the tree, of which I commanded thee,

saying, Thou shalt not eat of it: cursed is the ground for thy sake; in sorrow shalt thou eat of it all the days of thy life;

Thorns also and thistles shall it bring forth to thee; and thou shalt eat the herb of the field;

In the sweat of thy face shalt thou eat bread, till thou return unto the ground; for out of it wast thou taken: for dust thou art, and unto dust shalt thou return.

And Adam called his wife's name Eve; because she was the mother of all living. Unto Adam also and to his wife did the LORD God <u>make coats of skins</u>, and clothed them. And the LORD God said, Behold, the man is become as one of us, to know good and evil; and now, lest he put forth his hand, and take also of the tree of life, and eat, and live forever."

Genesis 3:4-22

Now the reason why we have these scriptures included here for you to read, was so that your mind could be refreshed on this matter.

Adam was made in the image and after the likeness of God, and what is Gods' form? God is Spirit, so therefore; to be made in the image of His spirit one must first be made spirit also. God then took this spirit that he had made and called it Adam.

You must keep in mind here that there are three parts to a man: the spirit, the body, and the soul; almost in a sense as the Holy Trinity is 3-part, God the Father, God the Son and God the Holy Spirit. Seeing that this is the case, if you were to take the physical body of Adam away then you would be left with the spirit and soul; the spirit being the essence of life and the soul being the essence of God within you that creates your identity.

When we look at the body more attentively it was stated that we were made from the dust of the earth; and in order for the spirit and soul to operate on this earth realm, God had to give to it a physical body; simply because the earth was made physical and *not* spiritual. Therefore; anything which enters and operates in this earths' realm must come first through a physical body.

For example, John 1:14 states **"And the <u>Word</u> (GOD) was made flesh, and dwelt among us, (and we beheld His glory, the glory as of the only begotten of the Father,) full of grace and truth."**

With this, He gave dominion to this body and the power to subdue *any* other form of spirit (that was not of God) that tries to enter into the earths' realm; and the body's covering for that of a spirit and soul is **flesh** and **bones** to conceal the spirit and soul within.

When we read Genesis 2:23 where Adam stated "this is now <u>bone of my bones</u> and <u>flesh of my flesh</u>" this meant that the two of them (Adam and his wife) shared the same form of being. As grotesque as this may seem to be to some of you, they literally were only flesh and bones, but they had a spiritual covering from God that protected them. This protective shield sealed off the flesh and bones from making contact with any form of danger. Illustrations of this are shown.

1 Corinthians 15:44 "There is a natural body, and there is a spiritual body."

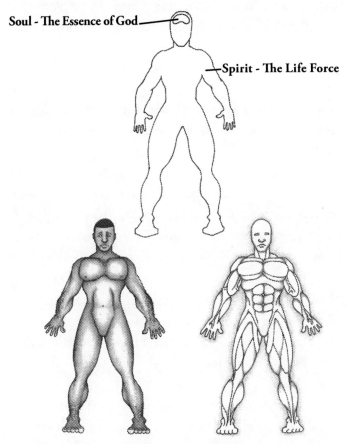

Soul - The Essence of God

Spirit - The Life Force

Man after the fall, is covered with "coats of skins," and hair, nails, etc. are now produced. The skin acts as the new form of protection, but was limited in preventing all sorts of bodily harm.

Man before the fall, is made only of flesh & bones and Gods' protective shield surrounds the entire body from all harm.

How is this discovery possible? Listen to the choice of words that were made by Adam: "This is now bone of my bones and flesh of my flesh." He never once mentioned here skin of my skins; but later down after the fall had taken place, the word **skins** comes into play. It is shown here in Genesis 3:21 as follows:

"Unto Adam also and to his wife did the LORD God make coats of skins, and clothed them."

When we begin to search out the depths of this word "coat", our minds are opened in a literal sense; because we are now able to grasp onto what this truly means. **Coat**, refers to something that is being covered and it is only covered once. Therefore; when it is shown in the scripture as "coats", it then refers to the covering of something, but it is done repetitiously. This then gives way to the understanding of when God made them coats of skins; in essence He really was making them "layers" of skin.

When we examine the human body and dissect it in its' individual parts, we observe specifically when it comes to the skin, that it is not one thick layer as it may appear to be; but "in fact" it consists of three separate layers. Those three layers are:

- ❖ Epidermis

- ❖ Dermis

❖ Hypodermis aka the Subcutaneous fat (layer)

The Skin Layers

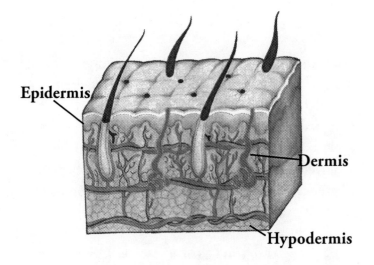

1. Epidermis – The 1ˢᵗ layer, which is the thin outer layer of the skin that contains melanin which gives skin its color and it also allows for the skin to be tanned. The epidermis also contains a protein called Keratin; which causes the epidermal tissues to be stiffened; by this it creates finger nails.

2. Dermis – The 2ⁿᵈ layer, which is the thick inner layer of the skin, which consists of: connective tissue, nerves, lymph vessels, blood vessels, sweat glands and hair shafts.

3. Hypodermis - The 3rd layer, which is the deepest and bottom layer of skin, is also known as the subcutaneous layer. The sub cutis consists of a network of collagen and fat cells that help to preserve the body's heat, whilst protecting other organs from injury by acting as a "shock absorber."

Now that we have gathered that the skin with its many functions is also known to protect the body's internal organs, this gives reason to show that when God had placed coats of skins on them, He was indeed replacing the spiritual protective shield that He had removed from them after their sin of disobedience. These scriptures provide more evidence to show that the flesh was our natural covering.

"And *though* after my **skin** *worms* destroy this *body*, yet **in my flesh** (the original design that was sinless) shall I **see** God"

Job 19:26

(Read also the story of Jesus' reappearance that was made to His disciples after His death on Calvary. This is shown in Luke 24:36-51 and this scripture will verify the accuracy of this flesh & bone discovery.)

With these two scriptures in mind, it brings you back to when Adam and Eve began to cover themselves with fig leaves. We believe that by this newfound discovery as to where their eyes had been opened; could it be possible that the flesh and bone appearance may have seemed to be peculiar in the mindset that they had *now* become connected to? Our reason for this is based on when they, after seeing the animals **all** with coverings, this then gave them the impression that they *too* needed to be covered.

Therefore; when they sewed themselves aprons out of fig leaves, it may have not been the common apron to cover the private areas as we have conceived it to be in our minds in these past years; but instead they could have very well covered the front portions of themselves if not entirely.

Stop for a moment, and visualize the apron that is tied at the waist. We are very familiar with this in particular and would find no trouble in believing that these were the similar designs of those aprons that they had made (with an additional covering for Eves' upper area) however; if you think further along, you will see that there are a wide variety of aprons.

For example, there are chef aprons that cover the front section from the lower chest down to the lower leg area, you also have carpenters aprons that also cover the front section however; only from the lower portion of the waist downward, but then again you have a blacksmiths' apron that covers the entire front body area from the lower neck down to the knees.

Taking all of this into consideration, it clearly opens this speculation to where there really could have been another way that Adam and Eve had covered themselves; keep in mind that it was never written in the scriptures as to the fashion in which these fig leaves were sewn and made.

With all this being said, this simply shows that in order for you to take in the fullness of this scripture, you must first be willing to surrender your way of thinking from tradition to that which may seem to be illusive.

Now that this illustration has been depicted, are you still under the impression that they were wearing what some say were fig leaves, to "cover those private areas of their bodies?" Or were they just trying to look "normal" when compared to the animals that were *all* covered?

The connection

Before the fall of man, God communed directly with Adam and granted that everything had remained as it was purposed to; this connection would have been possible for us in this present day.

Genesis 2:18-21 states **"And the LORD God said, *It is* not good that the man should be alone; I will make him an help meet for him. And out of** the ground the LORD God formed every beast of the field, and every fowl of the air; and brought *them* unto Adam to see what he would call them: and whatsoever Adam called every living creature, that *was* the name thereof. And Adam gave names to all cattle, and to the fowl of the air, and to every beast of the field; but for Adam there was not found an help meet for him. And the LORD God caused a deep sleep to fall upon Adam, and he slept: and he took one of his ribs, and closed up the flesh instead thereof: And the rib, which the LORD God had taken from man, made he a woman, and brought her unto the man."

This scriptures illuminates this discovery of mans' spiritual connection to God, and the way God was able to know what man was experiencing from within *instantly*, simply by means of an intimate connection that was made only by his soul.

We want to pause here for a moment and share an experience that gave us great understanding to the revelation of how Adam communed directly with God.

There was a time some years ago when my wife and I were in dire need of some supplies; and according to what we had been told those items would be readily available for us on a certain day. When that day came we were already at our lowest point and we knew those items would be able to assist us to a great deal from that point forward, however; when we checked in to see if everything was ready, they were not.

In that very same moment, I became very upset and I felt as if I had reached my breaking point. I then looked over to my wife and she was overwhelmed with grief. She then later shared with me that from within the very depths of her soul, she had cried out to God physically, but most of all spiritually in all desperation and hope of knowing what we were supposed to do; seeing that we did not have any other resources to take care of the situation that we were faced with.

I then got out of my van in that cold winters rain, (because we got the bad news on the road) and walked over to a phone booth, picked up the phone and dialed that place again. To my surprise, something had caused what we had needed to become supernaturally available, but in a short space of no more than five minutes from when the call was made. That was truly amazing!

I then realized that when my wife had cried out to God from the depths of her soul, it caused something to change instantaneously.

That day was an open experience of how God desired to speak to us. But after sin became present within Adam, all of mankind has been cut off from experiencing that direct communication that they once shared. In other words, we now have to go through the Son of God (Jesus) in order to get through to God. (John 14:6) All form of intercession must be made through Jesus in order to receive an answer from God. However; in those times of desperation when our soul cries out from beyond agony and despair, God intervenes, if not almost immediately. This is because we are no longer just praying through hope, but we are crying out to God in all truth, "**I need <u>You</u> *now* Lord!**"

We are most certain that many of you have had or shared in a similar experience as to ours, when at first the flesh cried out and there was no response from God; but when you or your loved ones' soul cried out there was an immediate response.

Given that we have grasped onto how the connection originally functioned, we now know why God said in Genesis 3:9 "**Where *art* thou.**" This reveals that when Adam and Eve received the fruit from this tree of knowledge of good and evil, in that very same moment the connection between Adam and God were instantly broken. In essence, this is why God asked where Adam was; not because he could not find him, but because the mindset that God had originally given *to* him was now gone along with that connection.

The curse of sin

When God first created Adam, he was a spirit and God gave him a physical body made from the dust of the earth and breathed into it then Adam became a living soul (Genesis 2:7). Hereon, the flesh was made to be pure and without blemish and it was protected by the spiritual shield; which in essence meant that the flesh had no sin and it could not be harmed. However; once Adam fell into disobedience this brought about sin; for this, the punishment was death, and because God removed the protective shield from Adam and his wife, and by placing a curse on the ground; He made for them coats of skins.

This skin was placed to cover their flesh and bones that was revealed, and instead of there being a protective shield that surrounded them at first to protect them from all harm, this skin was to now act as a form of protection. However; because it was connected to the ground and we know that the ground was then cursed by God, the skin therefore; was also cursed, so the same pestilence that would be in the ground would now be able to affect and afflict the human body. This is what brought forth the physical pain and death that we now are able to experience.

Aforementioned, this same dust from which God had made Adam, had not been cursed until that point; verifying that our original state and its virtue were now lost.

"And unto Adam He said, Because thou hast hearkened unto the voice of thy wife, and hast eaten of the tree, of which I commanded thee, saying, Thou shalt not eat of it: **cursed _is_ the ground for thy sake**; in sorrow shalt thou eat _of_ it all the days of thy life; Thorns also and thistles shall it bring forth to thee; and thou shalt eat the herb of the field; In the sweat of thy face shalt thou eat bread, <u>till thou return unto the ground; for out of it wast thou taken: for dust thou _art_, and unto dust shalt thou return."</u>

Genesis 3:17-19

"Unto Adam also and to his wife did the LORD God **make** coats of skins, and clothed them."

Genesis 3:21

You may beg to differ after reading the scriptures that reveal this theory, however; when it comes to those things concerning God, we must not forget to observe that our mindset **should not** be of that which is carnal, but of that which is spiritual. This is whereby the Holy Spirit _will_ interpret and reveal those things in which you read. (**Luke 24:45**)

"For *as* the heavens are higher than the earth, so are My ways higher than your ways, and My thoughts than your thoughts."

Isaiah 55:9

"Because the foolishness of God is wiser than men; and the weakness of God is stronger than men. But God hath chosen the foolish things of the world to confound the wise; (for e.g. the story of shadrach, meshach and abednego) and God hath chosen the weak things of the world to confound the things which are mighty; (e.g. the story of David & Goliath) And base things of the world, and things which are despised, hath God chosen, yea, and things which are not, to bring to nought things that are:"

1 Corinthians 1:25 & 27-28

CHAPTER 7 – CAIN AND HIS *WIFE*?

This topic is an interesting one due to the fact that there are so many thoughts and questions concerning this matter. These are mainly centered towards one specific question which is; if Adam and Eve were the only man and woman to be created by God, and in turn they only had two sons; when their oldest son Cain killed his brother Abel, after Cain was punished and sent away, where exactly did this woman as mentioned in the scripture (Cain's wife) come from?

Most spiritual leaders when asked this question usually stick to these two specific answers, which are: this woman was Cain's sister and this is because there were only two other human beings alive at the time, which were Adam and Eve (their parents), therefore; they had to procreate in order for civilization to develop. Others have said that God had placed this woman out in the midst of wherever he was sent, in order for him to have a wife and to procreate.

Now in order for us to find evidence of where this woman came from, we have to first research Cain and where he originated from; this is because your spiritual being gives significance to who *you* are connected to. The spirit is the life force, and depending on where this force originated from, it can then determine who you will become.

Let us now retrace the life of Cain and the heritage from whence he came. We will also recap on some of the scriptures mentioned in the previous chapter that gives relevance leading up to his life.

"And He (God) said, Who told thee that thou *wast* naked? Hast thou eaten of the tree, whereof I commanded thee that thou shouldest not eat?

And the man said, The woman whom thou gavest to *be* with me, she gave me of the tree, and I did eat. And the LORD God said unto the woman, What *is* this *that* thou hast done? And the woman said, The serpent beguiled me, and I did eat. And the Lord God said unto the serpent, Because thou hast done this, thou *art* cursed above all cattle, and above every beast of the field; upon thy belly shalt thou go, and dust shalt thou eat all the days of thy life: And I will put <u>enmity</u> between thee and the woman, and between <u>thy seed</u> and <u>her seed</u>"
Genesis 3:11-15

After reading these scriptures, we will now see the truths behind these revelations that may *not* have been known until this present day.

Everything that exists in this world begins first through spirit or a spiritual source.

"Through faith we understand that the worlds were framed by the word of God, so that **things which are seen <u>were not</u> made of things <u>which do appear</u>.**"

Hebrews 11:3

Having read this, we can now understand why it is that Eve bore Cain and Abel, whereas Cain was of an evil descent and Abel was of good and sought pleasure in upholding the things of righteousness.

When we see their mother Eve, we see the bearer of their beginnings from a spiritual aspect. This is because of what had occurred in the Garden of Eden. When Eve was created and brought forth to Adam, he then told her the necessary information that was required of them to keep the order of things. By doing this, as his wife she received what Adam said to her, however; somewhere along the course of time, she was then introduced to another way of doing things, and at that, a way that would set off her path to death and destruction.

By this, we understand that Eve had to receive two messages; the first was given to her by God through her husband Adam, and the other was given to her by Satan through the serpent. Since we already know that anything that will become present must first come from a spiritual source before it can be made manifest or become physical, it must first be given and *then* received.

We know that God represents good and Satan represents evil; this then, was the spiritual food that she ate of and received. However; Eve received *more* readily that which was from Satan, which was the root to causing Adam (who God appointed to be the Head of their union) to be overthrown. This is the first place where good was overthrown by evil. Because of this occurrence, the strongest spiritual foundation was able to affect the lives of her first two children.

Some of us already know that Adam and Eve brought forth Cain and Abel by means of physical conception, and with that, the spirit that was embedded in the womb of Eve prior to her conception, had already began to shape the mindsets of her offspring to be separated in their way of thinking.
If you think for a moment on the way that things are produced, this will further help to explain this very delicate but complex matter.

At first is the seed, to which it must be received by a vessel. Once that vessel has "in fact" received this seed, it is then embedded into their being (womb) and from this point it will be grown and shaped to carry similarities of the vessel in which it is being carried and from which it came. With this production in motion, and the specific destiny already assigned for these two seeds, the event that occurred later between Cain and Abel was more than likely to be inevitable.

God stated that enmity would be between **thy seed** and **her seed**. In this case the word "thy" that He is talking about is referred towards Satan. Although this may appear to be strange, we feel that this was also why Cain, who was the eldest, was the one to obtain evil first. The spirit that overpowered good was evil, therefore; her strongest seed being evil was what she bore first which came through Cain. Eve then brought forth the good seed that was given to her first by God, through Adam (from whom she was taken from, representing that of a good nature) but unfortunately, this was the weaker seed that came through Abel.

Now that we understand how these two were represented and why, let us cross-reference how this discovery is validated biblically.

"For this is the message that ye heard from the beginning, that we should love one another. Not as Cain, ***who* was of that wicked one**, and slew his brother, And wherefore slew he him? Because his own works were evil, and his brother's righteous."

1 John 3:11-12

This in essence links their spiritual origin that was later manifested physically, which also shows specifically to whom each seed represented. Now that we know that Cain was indeed from the **wicked one**, and he also gave unto God a offering that was foul because God had no respect towards it. This stirred up a jealous spirit within him, because God was pleased with Abel's offering and not his. This was the deciding factor, which drove him to kill his brother.

"And the LORD said unto Cain, Where *is* Abel thy brother? And he said, I know not: *Am* I my brother's keeper? And He (God) said, What hast thou done? The voice of thy brother's blood crieth unto me from the ground. And now *art* thou cursed from the earth, which hath opened her mouth to receive thy brother's blood from thy hand; When thou tillest the ground, it shall not henceforth yield unto thee her strength; a fugitive and a vagabond shalt thou be in the earth. And Cain said unto the LORD, My punishment *is* greater than I can bear.

Behold, thou hast driven me out this day from the face of the earth; and from thy face shall I be hid; and I shall be a fugitive and a vagabond in the earth; and it shall come to pass, that everyone that findeth me shall slay me.

And the LORD said unto him, Therefore whosoever slayeth Cain, vengeance shall be taken on him sevenfold. And the Lord set a mark upon Cain, lest any finding him should kill him. And Cain went out from the presence of the Lord, and dwelt in the land of Nod, on the east of Eden."

Genesis 4:9-16

It is said that Cain found his wife in the land of Nod, but we will first recap and begin to explore these scriptures that are given above.

In verse 10 of Genesis chapter 4, God said to Cain that his brothers' blood cried out to him from the ground, meaning that he was really referring to Abel's soul; reason being is because once his body had died, the only thing that was able to give any means of communication in that sense, would be by the soul that's connected to the blood.

In other words, your blood is an essential part in the function of life; Once the blood is gone from the body, the body will not be able to live regardless of the spirit giving its life force. Without the blood the soul will also be removed.

As we read further along, it states that Abel's blood cried out from the **ground**; the scripture then goes on to show where the earth received his blood. Following this, God goes on to state "And now *art* thou (Cain) cursed from the **earth**, which hath opened her mouth to receive thy brother's blood from thy hand." This meant that his blood was seeping into the earth.

These two words presented here gives clarity to show that Abel's blood was on the ground at first, **ground** meaning the solid surface of the earth; firm or dry land. It then shows the blood seeping into the earth, **earth** which means the soil and dirt, as distinguished from rock and sand; the softer part of the land. Once we understand these differences, we then move on to where God states "a fugitive and a vagabond shalt thou be in the earth."

With this specific scripture, we believe that this will reform the way of mans' thinking, and will possibly cause many to see the significance of thorough examination.

To understand what it is that this scripture is revealing, we must first realize that when it says **"in"** the earth, we have to take that literally. This one word alone that is associated with the earth gives evidence that Cain was not just cast away from the place in which he dwelt with his parents; but he was now being punished to live in or better yet **<u>inside of the earth</u>**. This was made possible because the earth now housed Abel's innocent soul by means of his shed blood.

Cain was now to become what many of us would call those from the prehistoric times, a "Caveman". Our reason for this explanation is very simple.

When God said that Cain would be a fugitive and a vagabond, He was telling him that he would no longer have a specific place of rest, and with that, he would be so troubled within himself that he would "in fact" be roaming from place to place, but not living on the earths' surface (Genesis 4:14) With that, God also mentioned to him earlier that when ever he was to till the ground, it would not yield its' strength unto him. This means that he would no longer be able to eat food that was created to maintain the human body and keep it healthy (e.g. by eating fruits, vegetables, etc. that were specifically designed for the body).

With all evidence shown, this verifies that Cain was going to be without natural food and he would be without a natural dwelling over the course of time. He would then begin to appear as some hideous being; as referenced in Genesis 4:14 "**and it shall come to pass, that every one that findeth me shall slay me.**"

Now the question to ask that will reveal this awesome discovery overall is, why would anyone want to slay Cain? This would be due to the fact that any human being taken out of the suitable conditions that are required for the means of survival; which means having the essential food and requirements needed in order to sustain the overall function and content of the body, would with time alter the human body over to an appearance that in the most grotesque and horrific manner could only be imagined by ones' mind.

Therefore, to say that Cain was a caveman would be "in fact" appropriate to the lifestyle that he had to become accustomed to. If we briefly think on the word "cave", its' definition is shown to be a hollow in the earth – especially one more or less horizontally into that of a hill, mountain, etc. When we observe the various rises that the earth produces, it forms shapes as of mountains, hills, etc.; nonetheless they are still formed from "**within**" the earth. This precisely, would be the only likely place for Cain to dwell. Whether in high rises or flat surfaces of the earth, Cain was to live *within* these places in order to be hidden away from those things that lived on the earths' surface.

"And Cain said unto the LORD, My punishment *is* greater than I can bear. Behold, thou hast driven me out this day from the "**face**" of the earth"

Genesis 4:13-14

Living in the earth was not something that was easy for Cain to carry out. Although he was of an evil nature, he still found this punishment to be too much of a burden; even much more of a curse (to which it was). However; Cain knew that there was power in what he said (proverbs 18:21) simply by what he stated "I shall be a fugitive and a vagabond in the earth; and **it shall** come to pass that every one that findeth me **shall** slay me."

Cain was literally speaking and even hoping to bring death on himself in order to get rid of this overwhelming burden. Yet, God whom was already aware of the mindset from which he was speaking with, then caused this *not* to be and to ensure that Cain should by all means receive and endure the punishment, suffering, and torture that would plague him to his death, as for the lost of his brother's life.

"And the LORD, said unto him, Therefore whosoever slayeth Cain, vengeance shall be taken on him sevenfold, And the Lord set a mark upon Cain, lest any finding him **should kill him**."

Genesis 4:15

We have now established that Cain's place of dwelling in the land of Nod was that of a cave. Which now brings us to ponder the question of who was this mysterious woman Cain found, and from whence did she come?

We believe that it would be safe to say that God did not create this woman, but instead Cain had actually found this woman within a cave. This would be reasonable to believe because Satan, who once again, still had full access to all his powers, could have easily made a woman in the fashion to that of Eve, but not so much as a companion for him as Eve was created for Adam; but specifically someone who was of his **kind** and **origin**. Whereas they could then create more of these same evil minded people to possibly corrupt the earth in a manner that it would be brought down to nought.

To justify this, if we were to look ahead in the book of Genesis, it is later shown in Genesis chapter 6 where God shortens the length of a man's lifespan from those prior to Noah, that lived to reach ages' ranging in the eight hundreds; whereas now man could only live to reach one hundred and twenty years. This was done for the reason that Gods' spirit would not always strive with men, for the land began to become overwhelmed by this wickedness; which validates the necessity of the flood.

"And GOD saw that the wickedness of man *was* great in the earth, and *that* every imagination of the thoughts of his heart *was* only **evil continually**."

Genesis 6:5

By these points that were made, it shows that Satan's plan was actually taking place as he intended it to be. In 2 Corinthians 11:14 it states "And no marvel; for Satan himself is transformed into an angel of light." Marvel means one that evokes surprise, admiration or wonder. Therefore the possibilities of this insight being true, is one that should be considered.

When we begin to think back to before the coats of skins were established, and Adam and Eve still had the mindsets of God and were walking in total obedience; we must remember that Satan intended to have evil commence and become rampant in any way possible.

His first plan which involved the fall of Adam and Eve from the righteous state to the sinful state worked as he anticipated. However; the remaining and most vital part of this plan was overthrown because God knew that man was moving towards the possibility of becoming immortal in that sinful nature; to which He *immediately* removed them from the Garden, to prevent any possible interaction with the tree of life. Because all of this had taken place and Satan saw where he had once again been overthrown, he after perceiving the countenance of Cain to be that of a bitter spirit; due to the fact that Cain always had to work at a completely different consistency from Abel, in order to receive anything worthwhile from his labor. It may have been that Satan saw this as *another* opportunity to make evil thrive.

Therefore; Satan approached Cain in the same manner as he did to his mother (Eve) by use of his spirit, only this time he *inserted* **thoughts** into Cain's mind, which to him may have appeared to be his own. With this, Satan also gave to him feelings of being underprivileged and treated lowly when compared to Abel, who had the benefits of having very little toil, if any, to produce a great work.

To confirm this belief, it is shown prior to Cain murdering his brother, where God had a specific conversation with him after the presentation of their individual offerings.

"And in process of time it came to pass, that Cain brought of the fruit of the ground an offering unto the LORD.

And Abel, he also brought of the firstlings of his flock and of the fat thereof, And the LORD had respect unto Abel and to his offering:

But unto Cain and to his offering He (God) had not respect. And Cain was very wroth, and his countenance fell.

And the LORD said unto Cain, Why art thou wroth? And why is thy countenance fallen? If thou doest well, shall thou not be accepted? And if thou doest not well, **sin** lieth at the door. And unto thee *shall* be his desire (his intended plan for evil), and thou shall rule over him." (Meaning that Cain had a choice as to where he could overpower *that,* which was evil and walk away instead.)

Genesis 4:3-7

In this passage, God had already seen the depths of hatred and jealousy that Cain had towards his brother. Which is why we feel that God had made this attempt to intervene on the matter; by addressing this issue that Cain was faced with. Yet Cain not being naturally intentioned to do well in that sense, made it easy to see why the spirit of heaviness would in the majority be with him.

In spite of this, we would like to address particularly with this matter, where God spoke to him about sin. God was saying to Cain in other words, that Satan lie in await for the moment, where he (Cain) would turn to receive a way to rid himself of what he may have felt to be favoritism and a biased display towards

Abel; but nonetheless the evil devices that he felt, *were* actually the desires of Satan. Sin who is Satan, as revealed, (earlier in chapter 4) wanted nothing but destruction to fall on the life of this young man. Once this was executed, despite the efforts that God made in order to save him from punishment; Satan knew that once Cain sinned against God, that he would gain an opening to bring this sinful spirit into the world again. Since it was not made possible for this to be done immortally on his first attempt, he would then do it this time but through the life of Cain by means of multiplying *his* "kind".

This brings us to the analysis of the woman Cain begat an entire lineage of evil beings with.

"And Cain knew his wife; and she conceived, and bare Enoch: and he **builded a city**, and called the name of the city, after the name of his son, Enoch."

Genesis 4:17

In our opinion, we believe that since Satan was very much successful in executing the spirit of sin in Cain; it could have been by reason of this, that Satan had created this woman. We have already learned that Satan has the power to transform himself into an angel of light (goodness); so why would it then be such a challenge for him to create a woman for Cain to procreate a legacy of this sinful nature with?

And with that, as we recall the possibilities of mans' original form being from that of Satan; could it not be that he now desired to use Cain to bring forth an evil generation with this woman.

You may now say to yourself, why could it not be possible that this woman was already made by God? Or perhaps, God created her since Cain was cast out and marked not to be put to death, hence giving Cain a chance to still have some means of companionship?

When we first consider this, we come to see that it was not likely that God created another woman prior to this event, because it is shown later in Genesis 5:3-4 as stated "And Adam lived an hundred and thirty years, and begat *a son* in his own likeness, after his image; and called his name Seth: And the days of Adam after he had begotten Seth were eight hundred years: **and he begat sons and <u>daughters</u>**."

This clearly gives evidence that no daughters or other women that came from the lineage of Adam was in existence prior to the birth of Seth; only after Adam and Eve had begotten Seth, it was during that 800 years where we see that they began to bare daughters also. By this time Cain's generation had *already* been established. With that, we must also remember that Eve was known as "the mother of all living" so this in itself provides evidence to this discovery that Eve was henceforth, the original beginning (womb) made in the image and after the likeness of God and for all of those who were of the *same* to come forth.

When it comes to the possibilities that God could have made another woman, we must realize that God was not in any way trying to undo the punishment that had been set forth for Cain. God told him that he would be a fugitive and a vagabond; this is a person who is trying to flee from a prosecution that is intolerable for them to sustain their level of sanity. It also can be someone who has become idle, irresponsible and wanders from place to place without a permanent home or any possible means of support.

Because of the type of punishment that was set forth from God. If He had decided to give Cain a woman or a wife to have a life with, this would almost seem to be as if He was rewarding him. This is because in reality, the way that he was now subjected to live, was without reason, no life at all. Moreover, God *is* just, (Deuteronomy 32:4) He would never purposely afflict another human being to share in suffering from a punishment that was not rightfully due to them. This punishment that was set for Cain was to follow through for his remaining days, which would cause him to continuously reflect on where he *once* was, what he *could* have changed, and mostly, where he would *always* be now; more specifically, being damned for the rest of his life.

To uphold this belief, the scripture states in Genesis 4:25-26 "And Adam knew his wife again; and she bare a son, and called his name Seth, For God, *said she*, hath appointed me another seed instead of Abel, whom Cain slew.

And to Seth, to him also there was born a son; and he called his name Enos: <u>then began men to call upon the name of the Lord</u>."

This passage gives evidence to show that there were no men, or generations that had been born into mankind that called upon the name of the Lord when Cain begat his generation. Only then when Seth came forth and his generation had begun to be established, was God once again glorified in the hearts of men.

It poses now a question as to, why was it that none was found in the lineage of Cain that called upon the name of the Lord? And if there was such a *desire* to seek Him out among them, what would have been the grounds for withholding them from doing just that?

Perhaps it was purposed that the Caveman (Cain's) life was aligned to join with the offspring from which evil came to be, this being, his wife. He himself in turn was also destined to return back to that from which he originated likewise.

A final point to consider whilst contemplating this matter would be that which is given in Ecclesiastes 1:9:

"The thing that hath been, it *is that* which shall be; and that which is done *is* that which shall be done: and *there is* **no** new *thing* under the sun."

With that being said, all that is left finally, is for you and nobody else but you, to determine that which you have chosen to believe.

CHAPTER 8 – THE BATTLE

2 Chronicles 20:15 " And He said, Harken ye, all Judah and ye inhabitants of Jerusalem, and thou King Jehoshaphat, Thus saith the Lord unto you, Be not afraid nor dismayed by reason of this great multitude; for the battle is not yours, but God's."

This scripture was specifically recorded during a time when the people of Israel had come up against great enemies and challenges that began to overwhelm them. This was because, judging by the many factors in the natural realm, their inabilities were a cause for defeat. Nonetheless, it was not *their* battle, and it never is because the LORD God promised from their time even to our day, that our adversity is not for our defeat, but for God to show us His prominence especially in our times of weakness.

With time, we come to face along the progression of life, trials, tribulations, set backs, devastations and many moments when we begin to feel our life is not our own. Despite the fact that none of us created ourselves, and that in it self should give us reason enough to see that we are not our own but with this, we belong to someone who purposely set out to make us great and fully capable of overcoming *all* of life's challenges that seem impossible to conquer.

However; we have come to the understanding of this world, where we are accustomed to the "you musts" and the "You cants'" and "that's not possible"; although society claims these things to be factual, the truth remains that with God, all things are possible, but *only* unto them that believe.

We would like to mention the story of Jesus and the Roman soldier. In order for you to gain a better understanding as to what will be said here, we ask that you first read the scripture Matthew 8:5-13.

This story specifically speaks about the sincerity of having a firm belief to the extent, that it can bring about supernatural changes in the most, darkest of moments. It tells of a centurion, whose dear and faithful servant, was at a critical point in their life and was nearing by minutes to receiving death due to the severity of their illness. However; it was with this same authority, that the centurion demonstrated daily amongst *his* men when giving orders, and saying to one, do this and knowing that it would be done, that he realized the most important factor with all faith; was by his willingness to believe and the courage to obey.

He saw in Jesus, the one true answer to saving the lost and dying souls; and because this opportunity was that of the same sort, he received in his heart and held onto his belief of knowing that once Jesus spoke that specific command to him, by means of his obedience, it *would* be established. We feel that this is why Jesus spoke of him with such great esteem, and with that declared that the faith that *He* had seen demonstrated by this centurion had never been displayed in the history of Israel.

By saying this, we believe that this is the most relevant illustration of them all, to overcome each and every battle that there will ever be in your life; and it all starts in your mind.

Your mind is the prerequisite that gives you the ability to think of something and combining this with all faith, determination and the love to make you foresee within your current situation, *anything* that you have set out to do, whilst operating in the laws established for us by God, *will* make manifest that which is the impossible. For some strange reason, we as believers and even the non-believers may sometimes have difficulty grasping onto the fullness of this concept; yet the simplicity of it, is what makes it great to master.

Can you begin to envision, the capability to "receive" in all fullness within your entire being, that which you have always desired to experience or even, the thing that you have been purposed to do in this world, is totally beyond the person that you see in the mirror?

Nevertheless, some may see this to be too impossible to hold on to, but it has been and will always be possible to each and everyone of us in this world, but only you alone can prevent anything or anyone from negatively impacting on what God has established specifically for you, and that is by standing firm on what you believe; and *remarkably*, it will change your outlook on life forever. This is because Gods' power is always without limitations.

To some, this is seen as nothing more than a myth, because of the odds most of us are faced with, such as prejudice to our ethnicity, our appearances, or even our level of education just to name a few. However; with just these few mentioned, they have been known throughout time to carry the "deciding factor" of where we work, where we live, and even to a point of who we are and what we are to become.

We thank God however; that these are *only* facts based solely on the wisdom of man, because when it all boils down in the end, all that ever matters is that if God be for you, who then can *really* be against you?

But once again it must first start in your mind.

Your mind has the ability to predict what an outcome will be, ways before it even happens. This is simply because of the **ability** that we were re-created in. We were purposed to be great, powerful, and to have dominion over all; this was because God himself, created us in His image and after His likeness. Therefore; it only leaves us to do the same as He does. When *God* speaks, things change. They begin to align themselves the way in which He wills it to be; and once this happens, this is where lives are transformed.

Romans 12:2 states **"And be not conformed to this world: but be ye transformed by the renewing of your mind, that ye may prove what *is* that good, and acceptable, and perfect will of God."**

God intended for us to be like Him, but because of the curse of sin, we were taken away from that. This is evident in Genesis 3:22 where it states **"And the LORD God said, 'Behold, the man is become as one of us, to know good and evil: and now, lest he put forth his hand, and take also of the tree of life, and eat, and live forever."**

We were already operating in the state of immortality but when we were contaminated by sin, God had to bring this state of "god" in us, to an end, because sin would then live forever and this is not what God had in mind. God had purposed for us to be with Him and to live forever, but not in a state of wickedness.

This is why He sent Jesus to redeem the lost, (that being all of mankind) from this sinful nature, so that we all could begin to know who we truly are, how we should live and *prove* **"what *is* that good and acceptable, and perfect will of God."**

God completes us, and when He begins the transformation in us to which our minds *are* renewed, its' almost as if we have come into a new state of living.

We can attest to the many times when we have thought on our previous lifestyles and realized how dead our lives were. Dead, is also defined as "resembling death or a deathlike state." which then entails that the mind is paralyzed and is not able to decipher that which is reality from that which is simulated (which causes it to seem as if it is real).

We chose to use this word specifically because, **DEAD** was "in fact" the state that our minds were in; and by no means do we mean brain dead as in "a vegetable state", but simply not knowing what life *truly* was.

We were alive and functioning, but not in the sense of the fullness that we later came to experience, after we gave ourselves the chance to really get to know *who* God is. Life prior to this discovery was almost meaningless. We both were only filled with the desires connected to a self-righteous way of thinking; even though we thought we knew what was right and wrong. This was because, we helped others when it was possible, but we still did not come to recognize that we were living a life that was almost too identical to most of mankind. It seemed to be something spectacular, but we barely noticed that it was not that at all.

This was by no means, related to being in a state of lack, unhappiness, or suffering from any physical or emotional means of affliction; but it was solely dedicated to the fact that we did not comprehend what "our" lives as well as others *should* really be. Because of sin, our minds were entrapped to think on a certain level of what is and what isn't factual or that which makes sense.

The world in which we live is sinful, and if we combine a sinful mindset and the nature of this world's state, this would only bring one to live **within the limitations** to which Satan desires you to stay in. This is due to the fact that some of us see things that *are* supernatural and we would call it magic, simply because our minds naturally, are in a state, where it is unable to comprehend why these situations are capable of functioning outside of that which we have been taught to believe.

Nonetheless, we all can state a moment when we wanted to know *why* we are who we are, and *why* these mysterious things can just happen. Whereas, the people of the world or in society will tell us that it's not likely to happen, however; these same people also *cannot* predict why they themselves, cannot control those forces that take us all from being in *total* control and knowing what is about to happen next.

This brings us now to the knowledge of death and life. Whilst we move about in our daily lives, functioning under only that which seems to be the supremacy to life itself, which is the laws of this world; we then deaden ourselves to a point where we no longer use the total aptitude of our minds, but abide by that which the *law* says is attainable.

So we unknowingly exchange the money, fame & fortune, and happiness for *that*, of the maximizing of our full potential, which *is*, our complete awareness and truly knowing oneself and most of all, reaching your ultimate purpose; this otherwise is used to be the *example* of a full life. Although money brings things and even fame at times, it can represent to be the level of one who has been fulfilled. Ironically, it later leaves many of these same "fulfilled" individuals, with feelings of emptiness, confusion, and feeling incomplete.

This is because for one to know ones' true self, it will *always* require self-sacrifice from within. Instead of being satisfied with the appetites of the flesh (e.g. comfort, financial security, etc.) some come to a point of realization that, this **cannot** be *all* that this life was designed to give. "In fact", it *was* designed to give you more, and that is of the truths to knowing life and the fullness that it brings.

This is what we feel the battle is. When your mind finally comes to the crossroads of life, "worldly living vs. purposed living" and it begins to frighten you to the possibility, that you have now reached a point where, you would have *always* known every aspect of your life that was to come, but now, you are faced with the fact of, *not* knowing that which is ahead of you. Although you want to know what life is and what your purpose is in it; this is where Satan will come in to battling with your mind.

He will now remind you of those comforts of life that you may have to forsake if you decide to follow through with your choice, but he too also knows that if you ever were completely able to give your mind over to the true power that it possess, the limits would then be limitless; but only by the Spirit of God.

"Now unto Him that is able to do exceedingly abundantly above all that we ask or think, according to the **power that worketh in us**"

Ephesians 3:20

It may seem as though this may be too difficult to grasp onto at first, but with time, it is revealed from within you, that only God holds the answer that we walk around daily seeking to find; our reason to this is because, many out there, including ourselves have come to know through experience, that He was and will always be *The* Answer.

John 10:10 states **"The thief (Satan) cometh not, but for to steal, and to kill, and to destroy: I am come that they might have life, and that they might have *it* more abundantly."**

All God desires, is that you would come into the way of knowing and by this we begin to live. We are transformed into a "new creature", (2 Corinthians 5:17) and we no longer remain in the "old creature" (or the old mindset) that Satan freely had control to possess. This is because, you would no longer be operating by what man says, but by what God says you can do and that is **all** things through Him.

You begin to experience the battle, when you have come to **know** that you no longer want to live life feeling empty and somewhat irrelevant to this world;

but you want to gain the true answers, to know from which you came and why you were chosen to be at this moment. Once you have set this in your mind, God comes in and takes over. He takes your mind, and renews it from that limited and doubtful way of thinking, and teaches you how to use the power of your faith to make manifest those things in which you desire; in essence, to bring forth the harvest of your purpose.

Although, this is a most liberating experience, it can also bring some moments where you may begin to feel overwhelmed. My wife remembers a time when she told someone before that 'it seemed as if once you've decided to follow Christ, and allow Him to lead you, all hell suddenly breaks loose on you'. This is the difficulty that most of us tend to struggle with: which are those things that we aren't able to understand, but we must deal with in order to mature in Christ effectively. However; this new way of life is more of a declaration for us, because in the beginning, God first said unto Adam, "Where *art* thou?" But now, when we come to find God, He then says *to* that generation of Adam, whom He created, "Welcome home."

When your mind becomes that of Gods', you will begin to conquer feats that men assumed to be irrational (foolish) to attempt. But many have come to learn over the course of time that God is infinite, and it gives to those that follow His direction, the ability to do the same with His help. He gives to us in essence, the mind that Adam had been created with, and with His promise we are destined to live this way through out all eternity.

Overall, we believe that in the sinful state, we are but only for a moment able to bask in what this *world* defines as "life", but with this is evidence of Satan. Since many are lost and remain confused even until the physical death, which then becomes an eternal state of hell and damnation; once you are able to grasp onto who you are and what your life means in this world, your mind is brought into a powerful state of awareness and discernment.

This can give those out in the world a chance to experience and know that all that they see is not all there is to becoming complete. This is where promise meets provision, and God will have the chance to bring us to the way He designed us to be primarily.

As far as it goes with the Kingdom of Heaven and Hell, this is not just one that is a figment to what can be imagined. None are able to say that it is not real, but at the same, many are very much able to say that it is. By knowing God, and that He is the immortal invisible God that many refuse to believe in, He never fails to show how real His presence is in everyday life, whether supernatural or natural.

"If any of you lack wisdom, let him ask of God, that giveth to all men liberally, and upbraideth not; and it shall be given him."

James 1:5

From the simple yet complicated facts such as, man in all his brilliance, is not able to reach the depths of the ocean, and at that not capable of telling where it possibly ends; to the fact that the sun which is a star, is yet the highest form of heat there is known to man and none are able to say why it remains positioned in the solar system; whereas the earth along with the other planets, all rotates and revolves on an axis around it without end. These fascinations only verify that by its complexity and our level of comprehension, once we are taken from the mindset of carnality, to that of the spiritual, we gain true wisdom through the Holy Spirit and Gods' mysteries are revealed.

"But God has revealed *them* to us by His Spirit: for the Spirit searches all things, yea, the **deep** things *of* **God**.

For what man knows the things of a man, save the spirit of a man which is in him? even so, the things of God knows no man, but the Spirit of God.

Now we have received, not the spirit of the world, but the Spirit which is of God: **that we might know the things that are freely given to us of God**."

1 Corinthians 2: 10-12

The Kingdom of Heaven and Hell may not have enough *physical* evidentiary support to verify with all certainty that it is a place, to which the human soul is destined to remain eternally. However; seeing that the human life is at times controlled by the individual, by which force is it then understood, when that same individual can no longer decipher the lost of this control over their own life, and to a point where they can be brought to face experiences such of misfortune and death?

The battle in which we begin to know, happens *only* when that person (or soul), allows life's truths of the unknown to be revealed; by opening their mind to receive that, which remains hidden from the carnal state of all men, they finally awaken from that state of sleep, which can only be described as deadly.

"Behold, I show you a mystery; We shall not all sleep, but we shall all be changed, In a moment, in a twinkling of an eye, at the last trump: for the trumpet shall sound, and the **dead** shall be raised incorruptible, and we shall be changed. For this corruptible must put on incorruption, and this mortal *must* put on immortality.

So when this corruptible shall have put on incorruption, and this moral shall have put on immortality, then shall be brought to pass the saying that this is written, Death is swallowed up in victory.

O death, where *is* **thy sting**? O grave, where *is* thy victory? **The sting of death** *is* **sin; and the strength of sin** *is* **the law."**

1 Corinthians 15:51-56

Final Thoughts

Whilst reading this book, you may have encountered questions that you may have received answers to and you also may have made statements such as "that's right" or even "that's wrong."

This is where you will learn that this book was not intended for right or wrong purposes, but to challenge you as the reader, by means of the revelations that were given here; in order to seek and **diligently** search out the Word of God, so that we as man, can receive a better perspective on where we came from as a civilization.

In our beliefs, we feel that if you do not know where you have come from, you will never have any idea as to where you are headed. So whether *you* may feel that we have evolved from another species or, we were created from a higher supernatural being (God); it is your responsibility to search and find out the truth as to where you will know what is your purpose, and how you can fulfill your life's destiny.

So as Ministers of the Word of God (according to 2 Corinthians 6:4-10), we pray that we have by all means, effectively provoked your way of thinking, and with this, motivated you to a point where you will come to find out the purpose that lies within yourself, to find out your true Source, and finally to become aware of where your eternal destiny truly lies. God has given to you "life", therefore; let the common ways of this life be released, so that the mysteries of your true being can be revealed.

The choice is yours!

"They that be whole need not a physician, but they that are sick. But go ye and learn what *that* meaneth, I will have mercy, and not sacrifice: for I am not come to call the righteous, but sinners to repentance."

Matthew 9:12-13

"And if it seem evil unto you to serve the LORD, choose you this day whom ye will serve"

Joshua 24:15

BIBLIOGRAPHY

i. http://www.Idolphin.org/Names.html
ii. http://www.en.wikipedia.org
iii. **The New American Webster Handy College Dictionary, Third Edition**
iv. **The Student Bible Dictionary**
v. http://www.dictionary.reference.com
vi. http://www.circle-of-light.com/Angels/ranks-of-angels.html
vii. http://www.sundayschoolcourses.com/angels/angel1.htm#hierarchies

AUTHOR-BIOGRAPHY

Brought up in a Christian surrounding for more than twenty-five years in the islands of the Bahamas, which is established as a "Christian Nation"; Ministers Darren & Asharan Paul have not only been taught the foundations of God from a tender age, but both made a firm commitment in their 3rd year of marriage, to accept the call of God on their lives.

They have personally gained full understanding in their experiences of "walking with God", similar to those of the days of our forefathers: Abraham, Isaac & Jacob.

By Gods enrichment on their gifts, they have taught with the assurance; as witnessed by many believers and non-believers, to carry great evidence in their lives, based on the power of faith in God.

They overcame surmountable levels of trials and tribulations; and by demonstrating their love through many uncomfortable seasons, they uphold true dedication to serving the LORD Jesus Christ.